hand in hand

hand in hand

CRAFTING WITH KIDS

Jenny Doh

LARK CRAFTS

Asheville

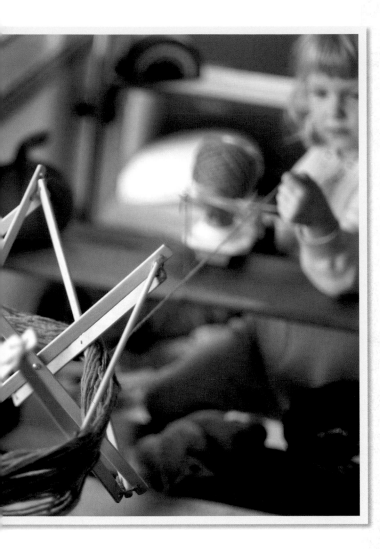

Jenny Doh **editor**

Amanda Crabtree **writer**

Nancy D. Wood **copy editor**

Amy Sly **cover designer**

Raquel Joya **designer**

Jana Holstein, Monica Mouet **assistant editors**

LARK CRAFTS

An Imprint of Sterling Publishing
387 Park Avenue South
New York, NY 10016

If you have questions or comments about
this book, please visit: larkcrafts.com

Library of Congress Cataloging-in-Publication Data

Hand in hand : crafting with kids / [compiled by] Jenny Doh.
     p. cm.
  Features craft designs by Jenny Doh and others.
  Includes index.
  ISBN 978-1-4547-0240-5 (pbk. : alk. paper)
  1. Handicraft for children. I. Doh, Jenny. II. Glassenberg, Abigail Patner.
  TT157.H3224 2012
  745.5--dc23

                                          2011031764

10 9 8 7 6 5 4 3 2

Published by Lark Crafts
An Imprint of Sterling Publishing Co., Inc.
387 Park Avenue South, New York, NY 10016

Text © 2012, Jenny Doh
Photography © 2012, Lark Crafts, an Imprint of Sterling Publishing Co., Inc.,
unless otherwise specified
Illustrations © 2012, Lark Crafts, an Imprint of Sterling Publishing Co., Inc.,
unless otherwise specified

Distributed in Canada by Sterling Publishing,
c/o Canadian Manda Group, 165 Dufferin Street
Toronto, Ontario, Canada M6K 3H6

Distributed in the United Kingdom by GMC Distribution Services,
Castle Place, 166 High Street, Lewes, East Sussex, England BN7 1XU

Distributed in Australia by Capricorn Link (Australia) Pty Ltd.,
P.O. Box 704, Windsor, NSW 2756 Australia

Manufactured in China

ISBN 13: 978-1-4547-0240-5

For information about custom editions, special sales, and premium and corporate
purchases, please contact Sterling Special Sales Department at 800-805-5489 or
specialsales@sterlingpub.com.

Requests for information about desk and examination copies available to college
and university professors must be submitted to academic@larkbooks.com. Our
complete policy can be found at www.larkcrafts.com.

table of contents

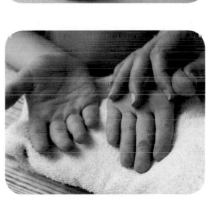

introduction

BY JENNY DOH

There are two things I know for sure about parenthood: One, that it is the most rewarding and fulfilling job I've ever had; and two, it's the toughest job on earth.

During the times when parenting came most naturally to me, it was often because I was teaching my kids about my love of creativity. Their eyes filling with wonder at the first swipe of bright watercolors on paper, their pure joy when we laid out huge pieces of craft paper on our dining room table to draw on, or their laughter filling the house as they made funny shapes out of clay were all moments when I felt privileged to be sharing my greatest love with them.

For me, creativity is what also aided my journey as a mother to retain my voice and identity. Through knitting, quilting, and other artistic endeavors, I experienced the thrill of being able to elevate and beautify even the most mundane facets of our lives.

The creative parents who have joined me to share their stories in this book, *Hand in Hand*, have experienced firsthand this thrill that I speak of. These incredible women are: **Jackie Boucher**, **Samantha Cotterill**, **Maya Donenfeld**, **Ali Edwards**, **Rachel Faucett**, **Pam Garrison**, **Abby Glassenberg**, **Cindy Hopper**, **Beki Lambert**, **Merrilee Liddiard**, **Jhoanna Monto**, **Jessica Okui**, **Ella Pedersen**, **Carly Schwerdt**, **Amanda Soule**, **Nicole Spring**, **Jean Van't Hul**, **Dana Willard**, and **Kristin Zecchinelli**.

In addition to their unique stories, these contributors share special projects that are designed with the entire family in mind. From felted bowls and upcycled bracelets to pillows, quilts, and more, you will find a bounty of projects that you can make with your own children, with step-by-step instructions to help all family members experience success.

The other thing I know for sure about parenthood is that our children do as we do, not as we say. It is by creating in front of them that they will create. It is by reading in front of them that they will read. It is by loving in front of them that they will love.

I dedicate this book to all parents everywhere, and the potential they have to conduct the toughest job on earth with love and creativity—hour by hour, day by day, and hand in hand.

amanda blake soule

www.soulemama.com

in passionate pursuit of creativity

I was such a shy child that I found great solace in reading and writing. Those pursuits occupied my days, kept me company, and kept me dreaming and imagining worlds far beyond my own. Creativity became a tangible part of my life when I was old enough to begin sewing with my paternal grandmother, Nana, who was (and still is!) an amazing seamstress. I would spend weekends with her, beginning with a Friday night trip to the fabric store for a pattern and fabric. We'd spend the next few days working on the piece, gardening, visiting together, and making food. By Sunday night, I'd return home with something we had

made together, and I always wore it to school on Monday. I treasured those times with her, and learned so much about sewing from our time together.

Though I never would have defined myself as an artist, I think I was always searching for ways to incorporate creativity into my life as a child (and young woman. There were so many little crafty projects and hobbies I picked up along the way and then would put down after a while. It wasn't until I became a mother that the passionate pursuit of creativity became such a huge presence in my daily life.

It wasn't until I became a mother that the passionate pursuit of creativity became such a huge presence in my daily life.

kitchen crafts

✱ **Soup.** We love to make soup together. It's a simple yet fulfilling meal that requires creativity, as we experiment and add different ingredients. Plus, it's an easy way to use produce from our garden in the late summer and early fall months.

✱ **Jam.** With a basic recipe, we've learned that you can make jam out of everything from the fruit you grow to the flowers in your backyard. As we create new jams, we also love to experiment and discover which breads go best with our new creations.

rhythm of our everyday

In the early days of parenting a little one—days that are so often full of the beautiful but blurry flow of diaper changes, rocking, nursing, and on and on—taking a few minutes to knit, sew, or write became a reminder of who I was amidst all the caring I was doing for someone else. I had a tangible reminder at the end of the day of something I had done. These creative pursuits became a meditative way to care for myself so that I could care for the little ones around me with a fuller sense of self and awareness. As time has gone on, creating has become a way for me to share and show my love for them as well. Creating things for my family, and for our family home, with intention and thought, benefits me (and my family) not only in the moment, but also in the results.

simple & successful family time

With five little ones, ranging in age from two months to ten years old, plus two adults, I'm always so happy to find the creative pursuits that draw all of us in to work, play, and create together. For us, this means finding an activity that's very open ended, to be interpreted as each person can and will, without competition. We have a tradition of Family Drawing Time that is so special to us. We cover the whole table with a large sheet of paper, toss out some paints or crayons and pencils, then everyone finds a spot and simply draws. Hours of family time together have been spent this way, siblings working side by side, getting ideas and inspiration from each other, creating works of art that may grace our walls for a period of time. It's an activity so simple and basic, but that's the beauty of it, and I think the key to its success for us.

Making music is another way we all create together. Having a variety of musical instruments nearby, from the more complicated piano and guitar to the simpler-to-use percussive instruments, makes it something that we can all join in on, regardless of age. A family making music together is such a special thing and needn't be very complicated.

our true, creative selves

I find that when we are all engaged in a creative project, we are truly our "selves" in the best sense of that word. Working alongside each other in such a way, we can get to know each other deeply and genuinely.

In order for creativity to flourish in my own family, it cannot be something that is forced, demanded, or required; instead, it's a gentle, long-lasting sense of encouragement, an open door, and nourishment. Creativity looks very different for each child. This translates into different things at different times: open-ended toys that encourage imaginative play from little ones; an overflowing dress-up box they have access to all day, every day; quality art supplies that are (age-appropriately) within their reach whenever the fancy to make something may strike; and perhaps most importantly of all, the time and

freedom in which to be creative. They need hours at a time (days, I dare say!) where they are not rushing around from one scheduled activity to the next, or staring all day long at a screen. They need time to daydream and create, and they need the empowerment (which we can give them as parents) and tools necessary to manifest those dreams.

rainy day crafts

On days when we're stuck inside, we often turn to classic board games to pass the time. Our favorites include Memory and Scrabble. Then, if I'm lucky, my children will request to make something with me on their days in. Those are my favorite moments.

a "first quilt"

As we prepared for the arrival of our fifth child, I was busy making things for tiny baby toes and a tiny baby head. Naturally, the older children wanted in on the making action too! Adelaide had a special pile of feedsack fabrics in her very favorite color purple that she wanted to make into a blanket for the baby. We came up with this quilt together, keeping it as simple as possible, and simply beautiful in result. She keeps this special one in her own room, "for when the baby visits." Since her little sister Annabel arrived, Adelaide and I have made a few more of these special quilts, each time selecting one main color and working with vintage feedsacks, to share with newborn cousins in our lives. Her pride in making a quilt is a beautiful thing to see, and a little baby all wrapped up in one of these First Quilts is, too!

materials

* Fabric scraps in prints, approximately 3 yards (2.7 m) total

* Six solid fabric strips, each 37 x 3½ inches (93.9 x 8.9 cm)

* Backing fabric, 39 x 38 inches (99.1 x 96.5 cm)

* Quilt batting: 39 x 38 inches (99.1 x 96.5 cm)

* Yarn or perle cotton

tools

* Measuring tape

* Scissors

* Sewing machine

* Iron and ironing board

* Pins and safety pins

* Hand sewing needle and thread

* Tapestry needle

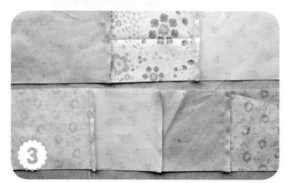

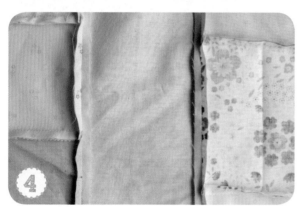

technique

1 Begin by preparing all of your fabric pieces for quilting. Cut the printed material (feedsacks, in my case) into 4-inch (10.2 cm) wide strips of varying lengths; 4 to 6 inches (10.2 cm to 15.2 cm) is best. Place these cut strips in a stack, in random order.

2 Begin sewing these strips together with a ¼-inch (.64-cm) seam allowance, end to end, creating one long continuous strip, approximately 260 inches (660.4 cm) in length until all the pieces are used up. Press all seam allowances in one direction.

3 Cut this one long strip into seven smaller strips, each measuring 37 inches (99.1 cm) in length.

4 Beginning with a printed fabric strip, stitch it together with a solid fabric strip with a ¼-inch (.64-cm) seam allowance. Continue in this manner, adding a printed strip followed by a solid strip. You should begin and end with a printed strip. Press the long seams between strips open.

5 On the floor or wide open space, create a sandwich of the quilt pieces. First place the batting, followed by the back right side up, and then the

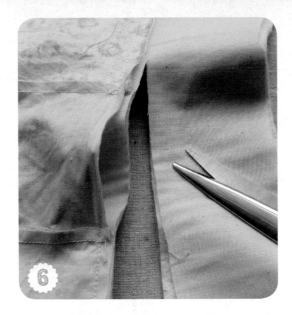

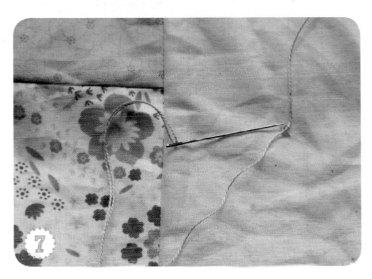

tips

❋ When working with little ones, I find it best to allow a little extra fabic for your project. In case of mistakes or the need for a do-over, it makes the whole process a lot less stressful for everyone.

❋ The degree to which your little one helps out on this project will vary with age, ability, and interest, of course. We carry a family philosophy that "there's always a way for everyone to participate." From the littlest one selecting fabric, to another sorting by color, another arranging in the desired order, right on up to the sewing, pinning, and ironing. Remember that creating with little ones is always about the process rather than the product. It's so much more important that they feel loved, supported, and encouraged than it is to end up with a "perfect" quilt.

❋ For our quilt, we selected a main color and pulled fabrics that we loved in that colorway, keeping it all visually quite simple (not to mention fun and easy for a little one to do). Vintage feedsacks are wonderful, but anything in your fabric collection will work.

quilt top right side down. Smooth out all three layers. (There's a bit of extra batting and backing around all four sides.) Pin in place around the edges.

6 Stitch around all four sides, stopping 3 inches (7.6 cm) before your starting point, thereby leaving an opening. Trim excess fabric and batting around the sides, being careful not to clip the stitches you just created.

7 Through the 3-inch (7.6 cm) opening, pull the quilt right side out. Press out the corners with your fingers. Handstitch the 3-inch (7.6 cm) opening closed. Smooth the quilt out and place pins or basting pins at various points through all three layers to hold it in place. Using a tapestry needle and a length of yarn, tie the three layers of quilt together at points

6 to 8 inches (15.2 to 20.3 cm) apart. Do so by making a small stitch all the way through the three layers to the back and then up again to the front. Tie a double knot. Trim yarn to desired length (I generally leave ½ inch [1.3 cm] tails).

maya donenfeld

www.mayamade.com

saving & revamping

My mom and I moved around a lot when I was very small. My fondest memories are of the flat we moved into when I was four—our very own space. My bedroom was filled with sunlight and my mother's creativity: collaged artwork, a decoupaged dresser, plaster of Paris puppets, handmade curtains and bedding, and a closet filled with thrifted and hand-sewn clothing. She even built my bookshelf, but what I remember most is what she pieced together next to that bookshelf. Made from reclaimed fruit crates, peg board, and scrap wood, my mother constructed a workbench with real tools and wood scraps. My closet was filled with a thrifted and hand-sewn wardrobe. I learned early on to save clothes for future revamping or deconstructing. By the time I was 20, my vast collection of saved and thrifted clothing was quite telling of who I would become as a sewer and designer. Now, with two rapidly growing children of my own, it's second nature to look at their outgrown clothes as potential for something new.

The word "creativity" often gets pigeonholed as activities pertaining to the arts, but every child is creative in one way or another.

becoming lifelong innovators

The word "creativity" often gets pigeonholed as activities pertaining to the arts, but every child is creative in one way or another. Sure, some are more intrinsically drawn to visual arts than others, but there are so many varied ways of expressing oneself. I believe it's a parent's role and honor to support their child's passions, so they can become lifelong innovators in whatever interests spark their creative fires. This is quite an easy and satisfying role if you share the same passions as your child, but what if they have a different path with interests that take you both into foreign territory? This is where we, as guides, are often challenged. Stretching ourselves to allow our children to embrace whatever creative medium gives them their voice is one of the ways we all grow, individually and as a family.

Another way I grow individually is by sharing my love of creativity with others outside of my family circle. If I ever have an opportunity to lead a group of children in a creative activity, we usually begin with a roundtable discussion to discover everyone's interests. Even the smallest child enjoys participating in a gathering when they feel that their voice is heard and valued. We then spend the day collaborating on a group performance piece determined by their ages and interests. The children pursue the area that inspires them most, from designing props and costumes to writing and performing. My role is to ask key questions at the right time to inspire them to construct their vision. I hope this process will give them the seeds of skills they need to become innovative and creative, by building self-confidence, teaching empathy, and working as a team.

kitchen crafts

I bake often, and there's usually an enthusiastic helper to stir, mix, or roll. My kids would be happy if it were always sweet, but we also make crackers, breads, and biscuits. My son loves cooking and baking and will help with anything in the kitchen, but he gets really excited about barbequing at Grandma's; our second kitchen really is her barn/home. She's an artist, nursery school teacher, and phenomenal cook. Creativity and delicious food are part of almost every experience my children have with my mother. We are all so fortunate that she's close by during her teaching breaks.

nature

My family is very influenced by the seasons and the natural world that is right outside our doorstep. I loved growing up in a fast-paced city, but I wanted my children to have slower and more rural experiences with the seasons, something I never knew in San Francisco. The long winters, filled with baking and crafting, are balanced by the intensity of our other season, known as spring/summer/fall (they all roll into one). We live outside during the warm months. Cooking and art mingle with fort-making, seed-planting, and berry-picking. It's a different kind of crafting and rhythm, and we look forward to it all year long!

transforming humble materials

We try to purchase items with minimal packaging, but some inevitably enters our home. Rethinking what gets recycled and thrown away has increased our stash of material to work with. I am inspired by the way humble materials can be transformed into something new. Re-inventing, re-shaping, and re-creating are my favorite kinds of projects. Cereal and tea boxes are some of my favorite treasures from the recycling bin. They make a perfect substitute for standard cardstock and can be transformed in so many ways. I also love that they take up very little space when stored away for a rainy day craft. When deconstructed, they lie flat and stack so nicely.

Many of the projects that I work on share a similar end result: utility. Although I always appreciate using something I make, the main joy and thrill are in the conception and creating phases.

the little book of BIG questions

My children have always waited until right before they fall asleep to ask really big and deep questions. This is quite common. It is a moment of quiet at the end of the day, and they know that they have their parents' undivided attention. However, most answers to these kinds of questions (such as: how are babies made, when will you die, who was the first person?) require thought and time to share. This special book is a place to write down that question to be remembered for the morning. It is a wonderful way to help the child rest easy, because the questions stop circling through her mind when she knows she was heard and that she will find answers. The book also provides parents an opportunity to discuss the answers together and reflect on how best to respond.

My daughter's book uses collaging of torn and cut paper on the outside and binding with strong thread through easy hole punching. As a six year old, she was able to make this book with very little help, once the cover and inside papers were cut.

materials

* Cereal box
* Blank paper, several sheets
* Art material for decorating outside of box (we used paste and assorted origami papers)
* Embroidery floss or yarn
* Charms or beads

tools

* Ruler
* Craft knife
* Bone folder
* Hole punch
* Paper cutter (optional but so helpful)
* Tapestry needle

ali edwards

www.aliedwards.com

invaluable & adjustable routines

In our home, routines are pretty invaluable. They aren't strict or constrictive; rather, they are flowing and adjust with the season and growth of our kids. My husband and I both work full-time and are lucky to have really wonderful childcare providers who both value creative, hands-on activities.

In the morning, we prioritize waking up earlier, so as not to be in a rush. We eat a healthy breakfast with protein, and we don't watch TV. We share a hug and a kiss and a "Have a good day!" as Simon gets on the bus.

In the evenings, we have time to chill after school. Simon can choose to play video games, watch TV, or play outside. We do homework and read. Because of my husband's work schedule, we're not always able to eat dinner together, but it's important to me that we sit together as a family whenever possible. We end the evening with a predictable bedtime routine, which includes baths, jammies, and prayers.

In our home, routines are pretty invaluable. They aren't strict or constrictive; rather, they are flowing and adjust with the season and growth of our kids.

telling personal stories through images

Too often we link creativity with arts and crafts, rather than looking at it more broadly to recognize creative thinking, problem solving, writing, and the like. Being creative can encompass so many things beyond a paintbrush. My son has never liked to draw or color, yet he's amazing at lots of other things. One of his favorite activities is building with Legos. He builds "by the book" and then will play for hours re-creating movie scenes. There's creativity in that play. My husband does not draw or paint, but he has a really amazing creative business mind.

For me, taking photos and documenting our lives is my method of creativity. If I had the opportunity to spend some time with children who do not craft, I would use photography to teach them about the world of creativity. I would give each of them a disposable camera and begin by teaching them something simple about photography. Perhaps I'd talk about how to frame a shot or about some element of design within photography that could extend beyond just taking photos. Next I'd talk about seeing your life through the lens. I'd show them some examples of everyday life depicted in documentary-style photography and encourage them to tell their own personal stories through images. I'd end with a challenge for them to document an entire day in their lives with pictures.

creative incentives

We've used picture schedules regularly with Simon. He was diagnosed with autism at age three, and we've found this very helpful, especially when he was younger. Picture schedules, whether they are drawings or photographs, are a great way to show kids specifically what needs to happen and in what order. For kids who are visual, this is a really nice reference point for following directions and for being able to see the steps from beginning to end.

capturing real life

Picture-taking is really a way of life around here. My son has grown up with cameras and photography, and my daughter is having that same experience. We don't make a big deal out of it and don't make them "look at the camera." It's just a normal way of life for us. My goal with the photos I take is to capture as much simple "real" life as possible.

My process often includes being an active participant in life, capturing images with my camera and writing the stories that go along with those images. I then bring those things together in a creative way, either with paper and glue or on the computer.

There's so much heart that goes into my work. I welcome each step of the process, especially the creative challenges, such as finding indoor lighting, discovering a unique story angle, finding a new way to write, and choosing embellishments that complement rather than compete with the story I'm attempting to share. The creative art of problem-solving is something I enjoy and look forward to when I begin a new project.

I love the process because it exercises my mind and my heart. The end result is nice—and it's a part of the legacy I will leave behind—but for me it's the process that is the most personally rewarding.

The photography and the storytelling that I do have enriched my life beyond what I could have imagined possible. I see everything differently now. I embrace the simple wonderful things in life so much more. That makes it all worth it.

rainy day crafts

On rainy days, Anna likes to do the following:

❋ Color in coloring books

❋ Paint

❋ Play with crayons

❋ Use playdough

Simon likes to do these activities on rainy days:

❋ Play with Legos

❋ Read a book

❋ Watch a movie

ABC photobook

The initial idea for this project was to have my son create an ABC book for my daughter as a teaching tool. The idea morphed into something we could all do together. My daughter ended up playing along by "taking photos" with one of our older cameras and doing some of the stamping. Both of these tasks seemed just right for her two-year-old attention span.

materials

* 26 pieces of cardstock, or index cards, 4 x 6 inches (10.2 x 15.2 cm)
* Alphabet stamps or stickers
* Small photo album for 4 x 6-inch (10.2 x 15.2 cm) prints

tools

* Digital camera
* Scissors or paper trimmer
* Stamping ink, if using stamps
* Pen for writing words
* Double-sided tape

throwing caution to the wind

I think it's important to start creative play as early as your children show interest, whatever that interest may be. That's easier said than done, though, with all the demands of everyday life. How I wish I would have thrown caution to the wind, thrown down a paint cloth, and let my kids paint without worry of mess or "ruining" something on a much more regular basis. Though we have had many creative adventures together, I look at how quickly they have grown and wish I had made art and creating in general a bigger priority in their lives. I also wish I didn't assume more free time was right around the corner, just past

that next stage of childhood. I've learned time is fleeting in all the many stages of children growing up.

Parenthood is a wonderful opportunity to instill a love for creating and sharing creativity. I hope I've instilled to my children my love and appreciation for handmade items—items made with love for loved ones. If they want to save some of the things I've made or, better yet, if they long to create with their children and keep the value of creating alive and well in themselves and their loved ones, then I'll feel I've been a good example of loving via creative expression.

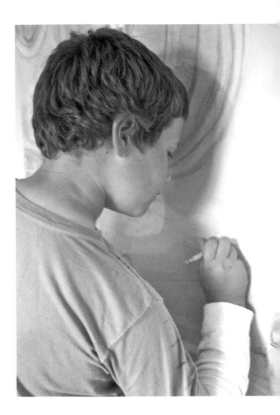

kitchen crafts

Playing on the chalkboard wall that my daughter and I painted is a favorite activity. It sits just outside the kitchen and makes for an easy way to express creativity and love for each other.

go bag

My kids are getting old enough to pack their own "go bags," but one of our all-time favorite additions to the bag was a small bottle of white glue and paper, for making sand art at the beach (sandcastles have always been a favorite too). The bags always include paper and pens, pencils, and markers for any trip anywhere, even still.

a connection to my spirit

Sometimes I wake up in the middle of the night with thoughts racing of all that I'm behind on—be it the laundry, emails, or fast-approaching deadlines. Though it would be wonderful to someday have everything perfectly organized, perhaps even with an assistant who could help me get and keep everything in order, I do believe that my lack of organization is probably what enables me have such varied creative interests. Embroidery, journaling, painting, collaging, quilting, gardening…I love it all.

More important than taking the time to organize, though, it is critical that I allow myself time to create. To be mentally, emotionally, and spiritually healthy, I have to have a creative life. In the process of creating, I completely lose myself and connect to my spirit.

playing freely

The great thing about being a lover of creativity is that I see value in everything. I love to create with scraps of paper, bits of ribbon, odd found items, and endless goodies. I've seen my husband look at me curiously when I pull things like security envelopes or other pieces of junk mail out of the recycling bin as he pays the bills. I've had great fun with my kids making crafts with all sorts of recycled items, such as sailboats out of milk cartons, and garlands out of muffin cups. Really, the list could go on and on of the things we do with scraps from our house. In the process of finding value in even the smallest of discards, I think we continue to fuel a desire to create as we realize each person's unique creativity and artistic gifts.

family banner

We have had a love affair with banners and pennants around our house (as has the craft world) for a few years now, and we keep exploring different styles and reasons to put them to use. Some of our banners are for specific occasions, such as family birthdays, camping, and the 4th of July, but we decided that we wanted one for daily use, something we could make together and then leave hanging in our home to enjoy every day.

materials

* Heavy cardstock
* Various patterned papers
* Glue stick
* Pencils, pens, and/or markers
* Other optional items: photos, watercolors, stickers, memorabilia
* Ribbon for hanging the banner (we used 5 different colors)

tools

* Scissors
* Paintbrush (optional)
* Sewing machine (optional)
* Craft utility knife or hole punch

technique

1 Decide how many flags your banner is going to have, based on the word or words you want to write. (We chose "FAMILY.") Gather enough pieces of heavy cardstock to make a flag for each letter. Determine a general size and shape for the flag. Our flags were approximately 10 x 7 inches (25.4 x 17.8 cm), but we decided to vary each individual flag instead of using a consistent shape and size. Draw or trace each flag shape onto the cardstock.

2 Cut out each flag shape. We like the homespun feel that freehand cutting gives the banner.

3 Once you have the flags cut out, it's all about gathering and adding assorted papers onto each flag. One good idea is to paint patterns onto sheet music with watercolor paints. Once dry, cut the painted papers up and either glue or stitch them to the flags.

4 Arrange additional collage pieces on the cardstock for each flag until satisfied, and glue or sew them in place. If sewing, add interest by varying the different stitch types. You may also

choose to add more embellishments, including photos of your family, buttons, beads, or stickers.

5. Cut out the letters for the banner from colorful paper. My youngest cut the letters by hand for a more kid-created look. Sew or glue the letters on.

6. Once you are pleased with each flag, use a craft knife to make a small slit in both upper corners of each flag. This is a parent activity, but you can make it kid safe by using a hole punch instead.

7. Twist the strands of ribbon together into a loose "rope" and thread it through the holes in the corners of each flag. We chose to thread into a slit from front to back, behind the flag, then back to front, so the ribbon wouldn't obscure the designs on the front of our flags.

nicole spring

www.frontierdreams.blogspot.com

In our home, we are surrounded by the beauty of the things we have created in one way or another, and that really inspires us.

a home filled with beauty

Creativity is just a part of life for us; we wouldn't know it any other way. My husband and I both had creative outlets and journeys we have been following since before having children. I think it's all in how you look at things. Even something as simple as making your bed in the morning can become art. I have to admit I am completely amazed every single day by my children and their huge imaginations and creativity. They keep me on my toes and encourage me to become more creative with everything I do. I am so thankful for that. In our home, we are surrounded by the beauty of things we have all created in one way or another, and that really inspires us.

seeking out handmade

My grandmother was a source of creativity and inspiration for me. She left us far too young, so my memories of her creating are especially important to me. When I was a very young child, I remember telling my grandmother what I wanted to be for Halloween. I had a very specific image in my head of a princess from some cartoon I liked to watch. There weren't any costumes available to buy of this princess, so she sat down with me and watched an episode, all the while sketching and taking notes. By Halloween, I had the perfect handmade costume to wear, and I couldn't believe my grandma did it all. I was walking on air that night.

Now that I have children of my own, I am excited that they also appreciate and value the beauty of handmade items. I hope that they always seek them out and prefer them to store-bought things. If they have fond memories of the times we spent creating together and the things I made for them, my creative efforts in their young lives will have been worth it.

creative chores

Our young children really want to imitate Mama and Daddy, so it's pretty easy to get their help; we just make sure to do our housework around them with intention and joy. We tend to sing songs as we work. They see us work, and they want to do it, too.

It also helps to have child-sized tools that they can easily get to. Our children have an easily accessible "clean-up area" that holds their child-sized broom, dustpan, brush, dusters, and aprons. We have a rag bag and our homemade cleaner (a simple solution of vinegar, essential oils, and water) within their reach as well.

familiar rhythms

Rhythm is the daily, weekly, and yearly recurring activities in our lives. There is something so magical about such a simple concept. Children thrive on familiarity and consistency. They feel safe and reassured to have a rhythm they can count on. Rhythm already surrounds us all, like the beating of our hearts, but nowadays it takes a conscious effort to bring it back into our home lives.

Just like Ma Ingalls back in the old days, we have a rhythm in our home. Our weekly rhythm is as follows: Monday is Baking Day, Tuesday is Craft Day, Wednesday is Drawing Day, Thursday is Handwork Day, Friday is Painting Day, Saturday is Gardening Day, and Sunday is our Day of Rest. My children always know what to expect and look forward to each day. It really eases their minds and helps them feel secure, relaxed, safe, and happy.

project

felted falling stars

My family and I make handmade stars every September to celebrate Michaelmas, one of the four seasonal festivals celebrated within the Waldorf community. A variation of felted wool balls, these falling stars are wonderful for indoor play. They are soft enough that you don't have to worry about your little ones breaking things, and they are also great for gentle baby toys. They're made with natural materials and are a great project for a wide range of ages.

Since this is a project for children as young as two years old, I sped up the process by starting out with a small cat toy as the core of each star. This helpful start makes it easier for little hands to create a ball shape. They also love the soft jingle sound the ball makes when it's finished. If you are doing this with older children or by yourself, you can skip the cat toy core and make the ball 100 percent wool. The materials listed are for one felted ball.

materials

* 1 small cat toy with a bell inside
* Wool roving—some undyed and some dyed in your choice of colors
* Liquid dish detergent
* Warm to hot water
* 3 yards (2.7 m) or more of ribbon, about ¼-inch (6 mm) wide
* Thread to match your ribbon

tools

* A large bowl or basin
* Small washboard (optional)
* Star cookie cutter, small
* Needle felting needles
* Scissors
* Sewing needle

technique

1 Wrap the cat toy in a thin layer of the wool, with the wool all going in the same direction. Use just enough wool to cover the toy. Add a second thin layer of wool with its fibers aligned perpendicularly to the first layer, so to help the fibers lock together when felting.

2 Prepare a bowl for felting: Add a few drops of dish detergent to some hot water and stir to mix. The formula of about 4 tablespoons of detergent to 6 cups of water, but the process is pretty forgiving so it doesn't need to be exact.

The hotter the water, the better for felting, but with little ones helping, make it just on the warm side.

3 Hold the wool ball in one hand and use your other hand to sprinkle a little bit of water at a time over the ball, carefully patting to wet the wool without dislodging it. Once the wool is thoroughly wet and beginning to cling to itself, start lightly rubbing the wool in the palms of your hands, rolling the ball back and forth. Once the fibers are matting and becoming firmer, give the

ball to your child and allow her to work it, using the same rolling motions. Have her continue this process until the wool has shrunk and is firmly attached to the cat toy, usually about five minutes.

4 Now rub the ball more vigorously in your hands or on a washboard. You will need to continuously sprinkle more hot water on it, or you may even submerge it in the bowl. If your water has become cold, add some more hot water. The ball should be very soapy, but not too

wet. The wool needs the heat along with the friction to be able to fully felt.

5 After the first layers have fully felted, add more layers of wool roving, one at a time, and felt each layer as you did the first. Adding many layers of thin wool is easier to work with than a few thick layers. Remember to add each layer perpendicularly to the previous layer. Once your ball is the desired size, switch over to a layer of colored wool for the final layer. Make it all one color or experiment with multiple colors. Your ball is done when the outside layer is smooth and no longer wrinkled. Rinse the ball in cold water to remove the leftover detergent, then place it somewhere safe to dry, usually for a day or two.

6 When the ball is dry, gather the small star cookie cutter, the needle-felting needles, and a contrasting color of wool roving. Place the cookie cutter on the ball and press a thin layer of wool roving inside the star, making sure to get it into every corner. Start needle-felting around the outer corners of the star shape and work your way toward the center. The best way to needle felt is with a straight up-and-down motion. For the tail, cut three or more pieces of ribbon about 30 inches (76.2 cm) long. Then fold the ribbon in half and pin the ribbon to the ball on the fold. Hand-sew the ribbon in place very securely. Trim the excess threads and let the fun begin.

abby glassenberg

www.abbyglassenberg.com

I think every child is born creative, and we all remain creative. But it is easy to become so self-conscious about our creative expression that we are afraid to dive in.

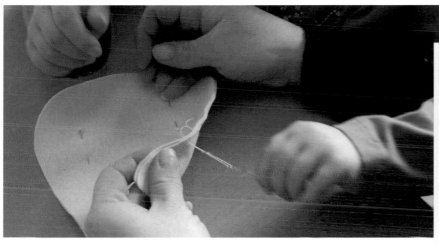

comfort in expression

As a mother of three young girls, my thoughts often revolve around ways to encourage creativity in our home. I know from experience how satisfying a creative project can be. When I am absorbed in sewing one of my soft toys, I am completely unaware of how much time has gone by. My thoughts drift, and I feel relaxed and happy. I hope that growing up in our creative household will enable my girls to take with them a feeling of comfort in their own creative expression, so whether they play music, dance, work on cars, write, act, draw, or sew, they will make time each and every day to do something creative.

supplies at the ready

One way we encourage a creative life is to have good-quality materials readily accessible to our children, so they can tackle a creative project whenever the mood strikes. In our kitchen, we have one drawer set aside for art materials: thin and thick magic markers, a big box of crayons, white paper, kids' scissors, glue sticks, rulers, googly eyes, brads, and masking and clear tape. My kids open and close this drawer at least a dozen times each day retrieving materials they need for all sorts of creative projects of their own design. I also have a box up on the counter that can only be reached by a grown-up; that box includes glitter glue, watercolors, stamp pads, and other messier materials.

Our recycling drawer also gets a lot of use. Cardboard packaging seems to flow into our house on a daily basis, whether it is a sheet of cardboard inside a new package of tights or an empty cereal box. All of the cardboard goes straight into this drawer, where they wait to become a canvas for someone's original creation. We cut it into shapes to make stencils, we paint and collage on it, and my children tape pieces of it together to make things from their imaginations. When the girls run down in the middle of their playing, grab items from those drawers, and then rush back, I never know what kind of handcrafted item I'm going to find in their rooms at the end of the day!

not afraid to create

I think every child is born creative, and we all remain creative. But it is easy to become so self-conscious about our creative expression that we are afraid to dive in. I admire my girls' fearlessness to tackle what I would consider impossible projects. My daughter will sit down and say, "I'm going to draw Daddy's office with Daddy at the window looking out!" If I wanted to draw an office building, I would be so overwhelmed thinking about how to achieve the proper perspective and proportion that I wouldn't know where to begin. She just starts drawing lines and windows and more lines and then Daddy in a rectangle and it's done! And because she was fearless, the drawing is full of life and charm. It is so hard to hang onto this fearlessness as we grow older. It is a healthy exercise for me to sit down and draw with my children, taking a cue from them and challenging myself to quickly dive in before I become bogged down in the details.

Not only is it good to work on quick drawings with my children, but it is also fun for us as a family to occasionally take on larger-scale projects. When we are looking for creative projects to do together, it's best to choose a project big enough for everyone to have a role, yet small enough that it can be completed in a few hours. Sometimes it's building the Halloween scarecrow with my husband, Charlie, carving the pumpkin head; my kids hunting for old jeans, a plaid flannel shirt, and suspenders; and all of us stuffing the clothes with balled-up newspapers. Sometimes it's baking a loaf of bread on a weekend afternoon. Projects that involve everyone not only bring us closer together as a family, but also show my daughters that creativity is the way to hold on to that sense of play—no matter how old you are.

kitchen crafts

❋ Every few months we make a new batch of homemade playdough. Measuring and mixing the ingredients for playdough is less stressful than following a recipe for something you're going to eat. If some of the flour spills on the floor instead of going in the bowl, the playdough will still turn out! Plus, the results are immediately fun to play with.

❋ One of the most popular dinners at our house is homemade pizza. I use a simple pizza dough recipe that takes just a few minutes to make and 45 minutes to rise, or I buy the dough at the grocery store. We all enjoy rolling out and stretching the dough to fit the pan, and then topping it with our favorite veggies and sauces. Sometimes I break off smaller pieces of dough and let the girls form their own mini pizzas to top however they please. Pizza cooks at 450° F for just under 10 minutes, so it isn't long before dinner is ready.

felt tooth pillow

For kids, losing that very first tooth is an exciting event. This project is a great one that celebrates the momentous occasion. The mouth on this little felt pillow is a pocket that can hold the tooth while everyone awaits the arrival of the tooth fairy.

My original design for this pillow was just a tooth with a big smiling mouth as the pocket, but when my seven-year-old saw it, she said "Oh, the tooth needs a tooth!" What a funny idea! The pillow is so much more adorable this way.

materials
* Templates (page 157)
* Tracing paper
* White wool felt, 12 x 18 inches (30.5 x 46 cm)
* Scraps of pink and black wool felt
* Thread
* Polyester fiberfill

tools
* Pencil
* Scissors
* Pins
* Hand-sewing needle
* Stuffing tool, such as a chopstick or blunt end of a paintbrush
* Fabric glue

dana willard

www.dana-made-it.com

deep yearning of the human soul

I think we often cut ourselves short when we think about creativity. Regardless of our interests, we all have a creative voice within us and a longing to create, whether we're aware of it or not. My athletic friend once told me, "I'm not creative; I run marathons." But *creating* doesn't have to mean *art*. Some women create organization within their families, some are fabulous cooks, and some create math equations and solutions to problems. My favorite quote by Dieter F. Uchtdorf sums it up perfectly: "The desire to create is one of the deepest yearnings of the human soul. No matter our talents, education, backgrounds, or abilities, we each have an inherent wish to create something that did not exist before. We develop ourselves and others when we take unorganized matter into our hands and mold it into something of beauty."

We only get one chance to teach, grow with, play with, and love each other. So I need to embrace the scene that's playing out in front of me.

a part of who I am

I can't imagine not making things. I think that creating is just part of how I think and how my brain and hands work. My grandma taught me to sew when I was 10. We just sewed straight lines on a brown paper bag, without thread, at first. We made simple little bags and gaudy '80s hair bows. And by age 12, my mom had shown me how to read and use patterns. I made all sorts of elastic waistband pants, simple skirts, and dresses for church. As an adult, I discovered I could sew and create from the ideas in my head; I didn't need a store-bought pattern. I truly find joy in taking fabric and turning it into something useful, or re-creating an old shirt into something new and hopefully cute. It may be an addiction, but I think it's a healthy one!

Coming from a family of creative-minded siblings means that simple projects, such as egg decorating, pumpkin carving, and making a gingerbread house often turned into lengthy art sessions at our house. We sat there for hours, decorating, coloring, and bouncing ideas off of each other. I enjoy that aspect of creative life. Even now, I often call my sister for creative input on an idea running around in my head.

kitchen crafts

Since my kids are still young, I let them help out where they can (without mom losing her sanity). They love to help me decorate sugar cookies, dump the flour in the bread-making bowl, and organize cheese slices on a grilled cheese sandwich. But probably what they love most is making scrambled eggs with their dad. They take turns beating the eggs and shaking in the salt and pepper. Getting my husband involved in the creative process with my kids is a treat to watch. He and I both bring different skills to the table and I think it's important for kids to learn from many creative people.

rainy day crafts

- **Cereal box dolls and pets.** My kids love to color. Every day they ask me to draw a picture for them so they can color it in with crayons and colored pencils. Cut open a cereal box and use the brown backside to draw a picture of a little girl or boy, dog, rocketship, robot, elephant, or whatever your child is into! When they're done coloring, cut it out, and they have a sturdy little paper toy. You can also turn these into paper dolls by creating/drawing doll clothes on a sheet of standard paper.
- **Handmade playdough.** Nothing novel, but it's classic fun for the kiddos. Search online for simple tutorials to make your own dough. Use cookie cutters, toothpicks, and forks to make funny shapes in the dough.
- **Nature crowns.** Make simple king and queen crowns from cardstock and let the kids decorate them with items you found at the park earlier in the week, such as leaves, grass, dried flowers. Use glue or sew them in place.
- **Monogrammed cookies.** There's nothing like chocolate chip cookies on a rainy day. Shape the dough into the shape of a letter to represent the child's name and let the kids stir and squish in the chocolate chips with their hands to create their initials.

embracing motherhood

I often evaluate my role as a mother, as I try to balance it with my creative needs. We all hear the cliché phrase regarding children, "They grow up so fast. Enjoy them while they're young!" And on days when I get too immersed in sewing, photographing, and blogging, I have to mentally stop, pull myself back, and remember that kids do grow up fast. I am a creative person, yes, but for this season of my life I am also a mother. We only get one chance to teach, grow with, play with, and love each other. So I need to embrace the scene that's playing out in front of me. Of course I'm far from perfect at this. The passions in my life are a constant juggling act: allowing myself to grow as an artist while also making sacrifices and enjoying motherhood. Bottom line, though: Will a sewing pattern or online tutorial matter much in 20 years? Not likely. But my kids will.

ornaments for any season

I love to decorate—decorate the house, decorate for the holidays, decorate for a party, decorate just for fun! Whether lavish or simple, decorations add that special splash of excitement to any room. My five-year-old daughter has caught the bug, too. I often find her draping ribbons and hair clips around her own bedroom, exclaiming, "I'm decorating for a party!"

To increase our party décor stash, the kids and I pulled out potatoes and paint and created ornaments for any season. Who said ornaments were only for Christmas? Now we can hang hearts, suns, clovers, stars, butterflies, and birds from our windows and doorknobs. Whatever the season, we have a decoration.

These ornaments are easy to make, adapt well to all ages, and have endless possibilities. If you've never tried potato stamping before, now's the time!

materials

* Large potatoes
* Acrylic paints in assorted colors
* Disposable plate or plastic lid
* Scrap paper
* Cotton fabric in neutral colors, cut into small squares
* Paper towels
* Twine or ribbon, 8 to 10 inches (20.3 to 25.4 cm) long
* Polyester fiberfill

tools

* Knife
* Cutting board
* Cookie cutters in assorted shapes
* Foam brushes
* Scissors
* Sewing machine and thread
* Chopstick or other point turner
* Hand-sewing needle

samantha cotterill

www.mummysam.com

joining in on the fun

Our two boys, Aidan and Marcus, tend to migrate toward the creative life when they see others around them absorbed in it first. An offer to sew something may get a big thumbs down, but if they look over and see me immersed in a sewing project of my own, they will often come running over begging to do a piece as well. I no longer ask them directly if they would like to create anything, because most often that is met with absolute uninterest. Instead, I find it much more successful if I "set the scene" first, and give them the freedom to join in on their own.

It's about joining in on something that looks like fun—it's as simple as that. One of my favorite things to do is transform the dining room table into

a little ceramic studio. Piles of clay sit around the table, and varying tools are randomly placed throughout. I start to tinker around with some sculptures while the boys are off in the background, and within minutes we find ourselves all gathered around the table making pinch pots and monsters.

One of my most tactile memories from when I was young is of my sister and me creating crayon drip paintings. With close parental supervision, we would take a crayon in one hand and a candle in the other. By carefully holding them together over a sheet of paper, we could make the most amazing paintings, made all the better because they were projects that involved the whole family.

It's all about joining in on something that looks like fun—it's as simple as that.

playing & inventing

Now that our boys are a little older, it's all about card games in our house. Toys in general seem to have phased out, and the boxes of cars and figures that once filled up the toy closet have been replaced with a precariously placed pile of never-ending board games stacked on top of one another. Though the games themselves may not be creative, we like to invent new ways to play them as a family. Sitting together on the floor, the boys will often start conjuring up new rules, and, with some input from Mum and Dad, they will eventually invent a new game full of the most creative ideas.

We also keep big rolls of craft paper on hand, and we'll often unroll it across the entire family room and dining room floor. Throw a pile of markers on the floor, and you instantly have an invitation to all

gather around and draw together. Whether it's working on one giant scene, creating a long game, or tracing our bodies and coloring them in, it's always been a successful way to come together.

One day a few years ago, my boys were interested in playing with extremely small animals. We decided that these animals needed some books of their own to read, and thus started an afternoon of creating a pile of miniature books out of paper. The books were no larger than an inch or so. There was just enough space to write a little letter or scribble on each page. What started out as a tiny project became much bigger in the sense of how it changed their play. I cannot tell you how many piles of these little books we had all over the house.

go bag

Now that my boys are a little older, contents that once included trucks and dinosaurs have been replaced with items the boys deem "cool" and entertaining. Here's the current list of must-haves:

* **Miniature sketchbooks:** The pile of books in miniature form are far more appealing than one large one. We use covers of sports magazines and plain paper to whip up a little stack of books with a few staples to hold them together.

* Markers and pens

* Stickers

* Dice

creator & observer

Though the little daily projects I do with my boys bring me great joy, my thesis work at art school still reigns as the most epic project I have ever completed. I hope someday to have the chance to revisit it and possibly go larger. With a concentration in ceramics at the time, I created an entire life-size room out of clay. The wooden floors (including the nails at the end of each plank), the furniture, the window, the radiator, and the fireplace were all constructed of stoneware. I drew the wallpaper and sculpted a few figures and a clock to adorn the fireplace mantel.

Viewers had the opportunity to sit down in the space and listen, as the orchestrated sounds of someone living in the house were played overhead. Within moments of entering the room, one would hear the "resident" coming down the stairs and going off into the kitchen to put a kettle on for tea. The feeling I had as

both creator and observer was one I shall never forget, and is something I will always be proud of.

Sometimes my own projects completely torture me through the entire process, and I experience many moments of wanting to just give up and start over. Some of them do indeed get thrown out. But there have been those that I couldn't seem to stray away from, and in the end became something so special and meaningful to me.

Other times there are works that, even if tossed away, were more about the process of creating than the end result. I recently worked on an apron piece that just never came together. After weeks of trial and error, it became one of those works that got put aside. Even though it never came together in the end, the time I spent with it had wonderful moments of experimentation that will undoubtedly be applied to my future

creative incentive

With my eldest son in particular, our best method to easily accomplish the assorted chores and activities in a day begins with a plan.

❊ We lay out a schedule ahead of time with the planned activities for the day. By allowing him to get involved with the planning of the day, he has an easier time accepting the "have-to's."

❊ Knowing what is coming ahead and allowing plenty of transition time has been key in alleviating much of the stress often associated with taking kids to places they dread going.

work. After all, any creative moment, regardless of the finished project and whether it's just me or the boys and me, serves to strengthen our imaginations and our family.

thaumatrope

The thaumatrope has been around in my household since I was a child, though, as one of the earliest motion toys, the thaumatrope can be traced back to 1826. This simple toy consists of two images on opposite sides of a card; the images seem to merge when the card is twirled. This is a quick and simple project that can be made with materials you already have at home. It is extremely adaptable, as it allows instant gratification for younger children, while allowing older children to make the project more challenging. If you like, it can be a great way to incorporate math skills and introduce some basic principles behind early animation.

materials

* Heavy stock paper (we love using large index cards)

* Drawing materials such as pens, crayons, and markers

* Tape

tools

* Tracing item (drinking glasses are the perfect size)

* Scissors

* Stick for spinning (we use colored pencils)

cindy hopper

Creating is when I am happiest, when I am truly being me and being joyful.

at my happiest

From an early age, I loved to color, make patterns for clothes out of newspaper, and sketch all the women's earrings during church. It is hard for me to actually put into words how important creating is for me. It is something I must do, something about me I can't help. Creating is when I am happiest, when I am truly being me and being joyful. My creative brain often keeps me up at night, as I lay in bed figuring out a new way to make something, tweaking a pattern or project to make it better, or dreaming up a menu for a party.

Not only is it important for me to create, but it is also imperative that I share with others what I have created. The share-and-tell aspect is important because I love to share that everyone can create. For many people, they just need a place to start.

different forms of creativity

Creativity develops in different forms for different people. From the accountant who creates a spreadsheet, to the mom who bakes muffins, to the artist who paints, there are creative endeavors for us all. It is about changing our point of view and appreciating and recognizing activities that might not outwardly look creative.

We are all born creative, and we all have a need to create. On top of that, creativity can be fostered and encouraged to grow. Allowing children to see parents engaged in all types of creative activity often piques their interest and fosters the desire for them to jump in and participate.

When my children are grown, I will feel that my creative intentions for them have been worth it if my children can be themselves and not be inhibited to express themselves. Most importantly, I hope they will be problem solvers. One of the biggest benefits of engaging in creative activities is that it teaches children to view and resolve problems creatively.

family memories

While I love to create something useful, things that make my world a bit more beautiful and meaningful are my favorites to work on. Designing holiday crafts, making creative gifts for loved ones, and producing anything that requires thoughtfulness really takes a creative project to the next level. Children get into this too, and it makes crafting more festive.

I can't stress enough that with kids, it is important to focus on the process. Allow children to experience the joy in creating, rather than worry about the outcome. They don't need a fancy end result to benefit from creating; there are wonders in what they can do with even one sheet of paper. In fact, a useful exercise for children is to show them what they can do with

very little. Upcycling anything also gets their creative brains whirling. They can come up with the greatest ways to use everything from toilet paper rolls to tin cans. Toilet paper rolls can be turned into a million crafts and tin cans make perfect May Day baskets.

Cooking in the kitchen always gets my family excited about creativity, and it brings us together. We also love the "Ding and Dash," so May Day and Halloween are my family's favorites. We cherish activities that involve both creativity and the family, because they make some of the best memories. And really, that's what it's all about: enjoying spending time with your family, treasuring making memories, and loving the experience.

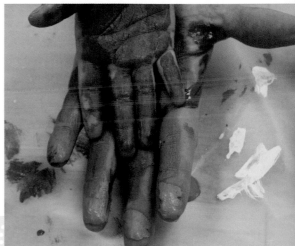

jewelry & key organizer

With just a few simple supplies, your child's artwork can become a beautiful and functional piece for the home. You can hang the finished organizer in the front entry or back door to keep your keys organized. It can also be hung in the bathroom or bedroom for displaying jewelry. During the holidays, kids can have fun making a whole batch of these to give as gifts to teachers and family members.

materials
* Small canvas, 4 x 4 x 1½ inches (10.2 x 10.2 x 3.8 cm)
* Acrylic paints in assorted colors
* 4 or more vinyl cup hooks: ⅞ inch (2.2 cm)

tools
* Drill and drill bits
* Small bowls, one for each color of paint
* Paintbrushes

technique

1 Prepare the canvas ahead of time (before including children) by marking pilot holes for the hooks, spaced evenly at the bottom edge of the canvas (we used 4 hooks, but you could use more for a larger canvas). Find the right size drill bit for the hooks and drill a hole for each hook. Prepare the paints by placing a small amount of color into a number of small bowls. Young children may find it easier to keep colors separated in this fashion, rather than using a flat palette. This helps keep the colors fresh; too much color mixing can make muddy colors.

2 Paint a base coat of paint over the entire canvas, including the sides This will be the background for your child's painting. Depending on the age of the child, you might want to do this step yourself or let them do it. This is a good time to talk about the colors they'd like to use in the painting. While you wait for

the background to dry (acrylics usually dry quickly, but give it a few minutes), you could keep the child busy discussing what they want to paint

3 Once the paint is dry, the real fun begins! Encourage your child to paint any design or picture. This is a

great time to teach them about colors working well together and other lessons about composition. And the great thing about acrylics; if the child isn't happy with the first attempt, just let the paint dry and paint another layer on top.

4 Once the final painting is dry, help your child screw the cup hooks into the pilot holes at the bottom of the canvas frame.

5 Hang the finished work on a wall and use the cup hooks to hang jewelry or keys.

jessica okui

www.zakkalife.blogspot.com

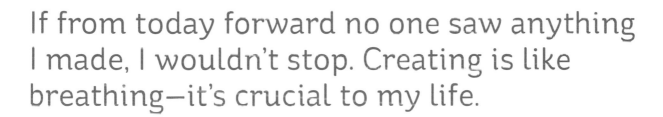

If from today forward no one saw anything I made, I wouldn't stop. Creating is like breathing—it's crucial to my life.

an essential part of life

As a young girl, I would make things with whatever I could get my hands on. Once, I made my mother some earrings out of paper clips and her macramé beads. I must have been about six at the time, but I still consider it one of my best creative moments. I've always found gratification in merely creating, whether someone saw my finished piece or not. Now that I blog and am able to share my

projects around the world, I have a new perspective. There's something very gratifying about being able to share my art with others and get feedback and encouragement. It's also rewarding to connect with people who like to create and share in my passion. That said, if from today forward no one saw anything I made, I wouldn't stop. Creating is like breathing—it's crucial to my life.

creative chores

To make chores more fun, I set the timer for a specific amount of time and make it a race against the clock. This automatically makes the kids *want* to clean rather than *have* to clean. Often, what would have been ten minutes of whining transforms into one minute of cleaning.

from brainstorm to reward

My favorite part about creating is the actual process. If I'm brainstorming a craft involving upcycling, I like to look at the original item and see what else it resembles. For example, let's say a juice bottle's shape reminds me of a jump rope handle. From that initial idea, I will plan out how I can make a jump rope with the bottles as handles.

If I start a project already knowing the basic idea of what I want to make, I use a different process. First, I brainstorm all my ideas on paper. I write out all the things that are associated with the idea. Next, I move on to drawing pictures, and last, I start testing them out until I get it just right. One of my favorite products was an eco-fabric gift pouch. It was challenging to come up with the pattern, but rewarding when I had a useable pattern to show for my work.

simple moments

My life is obviously still very much about creating, but it's also about building opportunities for my two kids to have their own artistic moments. For example, I have a recycle craft box, where I place items (the stranger the better) that would normally go in the recycling bin. Then, when they feel like making something, my kids can dig into the box and create. It's like a little treasure box for them.

We also love to go out and explore and try new things. Last summer, we played "tourist" and visited many of the hot spots in our area, like museums and parks. It allowed all of us to do new things for the first time together. We now try to do this year-round. Getting out of the house and seeing new things are great exercises for igniting the imagination.

rainy day crafts

Our go-to crafts for rainy days consist of the most humble supplies, like paper, markers, and scissors. Both of my children love to draw and can sit for a good hour creating with these tools and materials. However, sometimes they need a little creative direction, so I will suggest ideas:

❋ **For my daughter,** I might ask her to make cards for her dolls.

❋ **For my son,** I will suggest that he make a comic about one of his favorite toys.

❋ **Another rainy day pleaser is a large cardboard box.** My kids like to color them and use them for pretend play.

You really don't need much to keep kids engaged. The more basic the supplies and the more creative freedom they have, the better.

Coming up with new crafts and ideas is fun, especially because the projects don't have to be complicated to be successful. Oftentimes the best projects come from the simplest materials. And at the end of the day, as long as we're creating, we're happy.

paper roll bracelets

I'm always looking at recycled objects to see what they resemble. It's a creative game I like to play. Once I think of something, I try to enhance it. The toilet paper roll reminded me of a bracelet, and the project took off from there. I added the washi tape because it's one of my favorite mediums, and it's easy for kids to use.

The directions provided are just two ways in which you can make the bracelets. Children can choose their own tape and position it any way they want to make their designs.

materials
* Paper towel or toilet paper roll
* Washi tape
* Ribbon, 4 inches (10.2 cm) long
* Charms
* Brads, assorted colors
* Markers

tools
* Scissors
* Hole punch

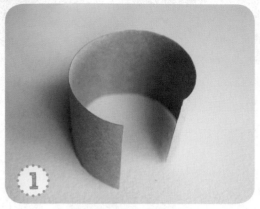
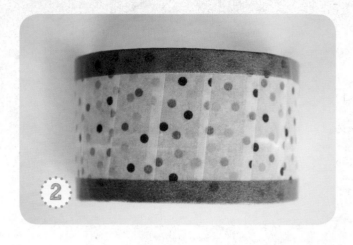

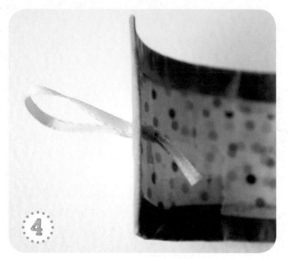

charm bracelet

technique (for charm bracelet)

1 Cut a toilet paper roll down the center lengthwise. Cut the roll widthwise depending on how wide you want your bracelet to be.

2 Apply a base layer of washi tape on top of the paper roll, and wrap the tape edges behind the roll. Add decorative edges with tape of a contrasting color.

3 Cut a piece of ribbon about 4 inches (10.2 cm) long (this will vary depending on how wide the bracelet is). Tie a charm to the center of the ribbon. Tape one end of the ribbon to the back side of the bracelet. Wrap the ribbon around the front and back again, with the charm positioned on the front. Tape the other end of the ribbon to the back.

4 To make the clasp for the charm bracelet:

- Punch a hole on one end and attach a decorative brad.
- Punch a hole on the opposite end and thread a folded and knotted piece of ribbon through the hole.
- Loop the ribbon over the brad to secure the bracelet. Cover the entire back side of the bracelet with washi tape.

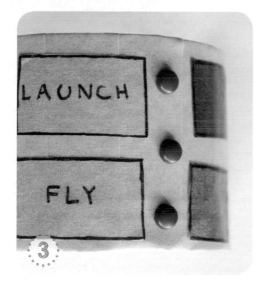

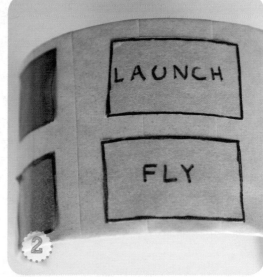

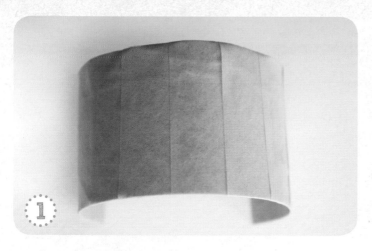

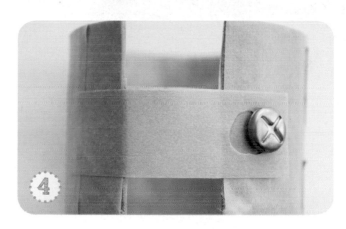

rocket bracelet

technique (for rocket bracelet)

1 Cut a toilet paper roll down the center lengthwise. Cut the roll widthwise depending on how wide you want your bracelet to be. Apply a base layer of washi tape on top, and wrap the tape edges behind the roll.

2 Cut six rectangles from bits of washi tape to make "buttons" and outline them all with black marker. Label two of them "Launch" and "Fly," and stick those in the center of the bracelet. Stick the remaining buttons on both sides of the word buttons.

3 Punch three holes on each side of the word buttons and push decorative brads into the holes.

4 To make the clasp for the rocket bracelet:

- Cut a 3-inch (7.6 cm) piece of washi tape and stick it on one end of the bracelet, on the top. Fold it over in half, so the sticky sides are together and the remaining sticky part is taped on the back of the rocket bracelet.

- Punch a hole at the folded edge of the flap you just created.
- Punch a second hole on the opposite side of bracelet. Add a decorative brad.
- Hook the punched hole over the brad to secure the bracelet. Cover the entire back side of the bracelet with washi tape.

carly schwerdt

www.neststudio.com.au

One of my first memories of creating is of drawing flowers by the window in my bedroom, so I love watching my girls enjoy the same experience.

embracing personal creativity

Although I have been creative all my life, I didn't really embrace it until I was pregnant with my oldest daughter, Lily. I had even studied visual communications in college, but still didn't feel terribly creative. Once I was pregnant, however, I really began to give in to that urge to not just be creative, but to actually make things, crafty things. I sewed toys, made clothes, crocheted a baby bonnet—whatever I pleased.

At the time it felt like an odd thing to do, to make things for my family and me rather than do something creative professionally, but something opened up the floodgates during that pregnancy. Now, those gates have truly blown off, nowhere to be seen again. I just simply can't imagine life without that freedom to express my own ideas. I can't even go for a coffee without a pencil and paper. It is pure agony to find myself caught without at least a pen and even a receipt; at times, I have drawn important ideas on the back of a receipt.

go bag

I am a big fan of my children using what they have to entertain themselves. That, in itself, is a fabulous tool for teaching creativity.

❋ **At the beach,** my girls love to have only a bucket and a shovel. Since we live near the beach, those items are always in the trunk of the car. Lily makes magnificent sand drawings of mermaids with just her imagination and a shovel.

❋ **At the park,** we often bring a ball to play with, but my girls are too busy looking for garden fairies to play with it.

❋ **At the pool,** the girls love using their goggles for underwater creative adventures.

❋ **At the café,** we often stay entertained with a pencil and paper, or a handful of Legos. If I know we might be somewhere for a long time, I will also bring an illustrated pack of cards, like Go Fish.

❋ **In the car,** both the girls have travel folders that open out like little tables. Inside the folders are pencils, paper, scissors, and whatever else they cram in there. I am not too fussy about messes, so this helps me relax if the girls bring toys like dolls and doll clothes into the car.

allowing yourself time to play

When I think about art, I believe that you don't need a degree, a course, or even a book to be successful. You just need a pencil and paper, dirt and seeds, flour and water, or whatever else you'd like. You also need to give yourself the time to play, without caring what it looks like. Creativity comes in many forms, from cooking dinner to cleaning house. The finished product doesn't need to be a masterpiece.

When I'm keeping this in mind for my girls, I like to just let them be, even if it means they seem bored at first. But giving them the time and freedom to play, experiment, and even fail helps them learn. So we have a box of beautiful sharp pencils and a pile of fresh paper by the dining room table, always ready and waiting for anyone who wishes to do some drawing. Usually Lily, who is now seven years old, is calling out for "Family Draw Time," where we all sit and sketch. Sometimes we decide upon a theme, like a family member or favorite animal, to make it even more fun.

remembering the good & the bad

One of my first memories of creating is of drawing flowers by the window in my bedroom, so I love watching my girls enjoy the same experience. I also remember seeing homemade playdough for the first time on the fist day of kindergarten; I never wanted to go home! I spent plenty of time hanging out in my aunt's art room (she was an art teacher), where I had the chance to play with all of her fun supplies. And I vividly recall the smell of my first tin of Faber-Castell pencils, which I still have.

Though I've had plenty of great crafting moments, I've also had my share of moments that didn't go as planned. One night, I found myself desperate to finish a sewing project. No reason, I just had to finish. I was sewing along and all of a sudden the needle went straight through my thumb. I was in so much shock that I couldn't feel the pain for at least five minutes. And another experience that I have to laugh at now: The day before an exhibition I was helping my friend Amy with her screen-printing. My job was to mix the ink, which I did—so well, in fact, that the bowl I was mixing with slipped from my hand. As if in slow motion, it flew through the air, causing very large dollops of ink to land smack in the middle of Amy's perfectly printed final works! Just like any experience, though, the times that don't go as planned make the moments that go even better than planned that much more enjoyable.

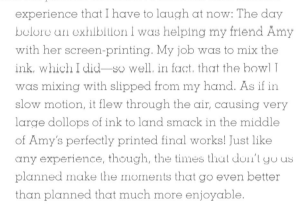

project

painted paper lampshade

I first made these pretty lampshades with my daughter Lily when she was three years old, to decorate my shop for an exhibition (they were meant to look like hot air balloons). We had so much fun and they looked so fabulous that they stayed there for two years until we moved.

This project is perfect in so many ways. Not only is it suitable for children of any age and adults alike, but it is also very inexpensive. And to top all that off, it looks brilliant, so hanging it in the home will brighten up the space and brighten up the heart of the little artist who made it.

materials

* Paper lampshade (we used the IKEA Regolit pendant lampshade)

* 2 jars of water

* Watercolor paint set, tubes and a palette (or premixed jars of color)

tools

* Newspaper or oilcloth (to keep workspace clean)

* Bowl to serve as a base for the lamp shade

* Watercolor brushes (soft and fine)

project

technique

1 Prepare your workspace with some newspaper or oilcloth.

2 Pop your lampshade on top of the bowl so it doesn't roll away. Have your water jars ready: one for washing the brush and one for using while mixing colors.

3 You might like to practice some designs on paper first, but most children will want to jump right into this exciting project. It's not often they get to paint the furniture.

4 Paint directly onto the paper lamp shade. You'll want to use plenty of water but not so much that you tear the paper. It may take just a few minutes of practice to find the right balance.

5 Once the paint is dry, your beautiful pieces are ready to hang.

tips

✳ Watercolors need little cleaning up. Leave your palette to dry, wash out your jars and brushes, wipe the table, wash your bowl, and you are finished.

✳ If your child is finding the watercolors a challenge, then switch them over to regular acrylic paint.

✳ For a stunning effect, paint several lamp shades and cluster them together in odd numbers and varying sizes.

✳ If you are stuck for painting ideas, why not take inspiration from your favorite fabric?

✳ This project would be equally as fun with tissue paper, Japanese rice paper, and a pot of papier-mâché paste. Simply make sure your paper has plenty of paste brushed on, and lay it onto the lantern, gently smoothing out the crinkles. Keep going until the lampshade is covered.

jackie boucher

www.living.weelife.com

a beautiful give-and-take

Even with a degree in psychology and criminology, I somehow ended up in a creative field. Not too surprising, I suppose, when I think back about what my aptitudes were growing up. Now I am one happy graphic designer, and I've had some life-altering gigs because of that. My proudest ones were leading a small but incredible design team for our local NHL hockey team and being on a team of fantastic designers who created the look of the Games for the Vancouver 2010 Olympic and Paralympic Winter Games.

Like any job, however, you are often doing the work for someone else, with someone else's constraints. I always want to do more and try new things to round out my creative life. Having a child has given me permission, so to speak, to try my hand in endless creative projects, just for the fun of it. I really value that. I always feel like I've only just begun when it comes to creating. And that is really exciting. This idea is what led me to start my blog and to dabble in the world of fabric design.

Having a child has given me permission, so to speak, to try my hand in endless creative projects, just for the fun of it.

finding a balance

When you love the process of creating something, and it turns out more amazing than you thought it would, it is magical. But even without that fantastic product, the process is what's important. If I don't like doing it, then it's not worth it to me, no matter how cute the outcome is. Sometimes, I use crafting as just an excuse for learning. In that case, the end product doesn't matter as much, as long as we had a chance to learn something while playing and expressing ourselves. For example, when my son, Spenser, started getting interested in Ancient Egypt and we decided it would be the theme for his sixth birthday party, I took the opportunity to find Egyptology-themed crafty projects for weeks before the party. We all learned a lot about hieroglyphics, papyrus, and the Nile.

Some of my favorite creative projects have been fun, educational, and also arose out of no planning on my part. During the 2010 Winter Games, Spenser started to show an interest in the flags of different nations. I brought home a little book from work that depicted each flag of all the participating nations, and he quickly came up with his own crafty idea of making his own flags with straws, paper, and crayons.

With any project, creativity is about finding that balance between inflow and outflow. I can't have one without the other, and I have to remind myself of that regularly. I can spend a whole day at the art gallery, at the library, or on the web looking for inspiration, but if I don't actually sit down and start outputting, I can get stuck. Likewise, there are days when I sit and stare at that proverbial blank canvas and no amount of forcing makes good things happen. It's about disciplining myself to do both in balance.

go bag

* We always carry a sketchbook with a handful of colored pencils or markers; it's simple, but it's the one constant in our bag. Spenser is almost always up for drawing his latest invention or the next imaginary place on his mind. In a pinch, there's always tic-tac-toe, where we change the "X's" and "O's" to more interesting creatures or symbols.

* To mix it up a bit, we like to bring one of Taro Gomi's genius coloring books. It's way more than practicing your ability to keep in the lines; instead, it encourages you to contribute your own ideas to the drawing.

* I love making up scavenger hunts to take along when camping or playing at the park. They not only keep us occupied, but they also hone important observation skills, important in creative life and beyond.

* Bringing white glue and paper to the beach means we can whip up some sand art with a moment's notice.

* For camping, I love bringing paints. There are so many things you can do with them, and what better place to embark on messy projects than outside?

individual creativity

Creativity is so much more than putting paint to paper; it's also about using our imaginations and hatching ideas. Spenser has shown more aptitude in using words and imagination than in colored pencils. From the time he could hold a crayon, I was putting paper in front of him, along with what I thought was an enticing selection of crayons to choose from. Nine times out of ten, if I gave him white paper, he would grab the white crayon and get to work. And the coloring happened only when he took a break from organizing the crayons first. He would place each crayon, one by one, onto the floor, lining them up carefully. Then, he would take each crayon and put them back on the table, again making sure they were lined up.

The process bewildered me at first. I tried all sorts of cajoling, but he still seemed to prefer organizing crayons to drawing with them. And with his white-on-white creations, I had to assume he had a very "subtle" aesthetic. Then I had what I thought was a brilliant idea: How cool would a white crayon look on an orange piece of paper? So, down goes an orange piece of paper in front of him. You guessed it— he grabs the orange crayon. A black piece of paper: a

black crayon. This went on in some degree for a couple years. Now, at age six, while he seems fine with using a contrasting paint or marker, he will usually use only one color per piece, unless he is reminded that he has more options.

So I think everyone has at least some level of creativity in them that can either be nurtured, or, in extreme cases, hampered. In Spenser's case, a creativity killer would be to focus too much on the outcome of the endeavor and not enough on the process. Instead of gushing over Spenser's choice of colors, for example, I prefer to talk about his technique. I also might comment on how much effort he appeared to put into it or comment if he tried something new. This approach highlights the value of hard work and risk-taking rather than the finished product.

kitchen crafts

* Right now Spenser's favorite kitchen thing to do is make whipped cream. We are trying to limit it to once a week, but it's not easy. We use a carton of whipping cream that has cream as its only ingredient, and Spenser loves to use the electric beater to whip up a batch. I love that we can control the sugar amounts. So far his creations include putting it on top of a glass of orange juice for his visiting grandma and accompanying it with a bowl of strawberries with cut-up chocolate bars on top for dessert.

* We also love to make edible playdough.

* We pick up a kid-friendly cookbook at the library. Spencer chooses a meal, we make up the grocery list and do the shopping together. He's more likely to try new foods when he is involved in the process.

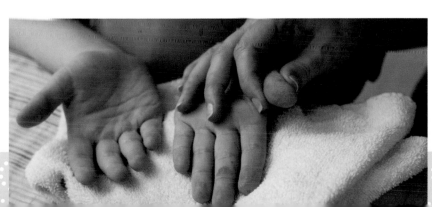

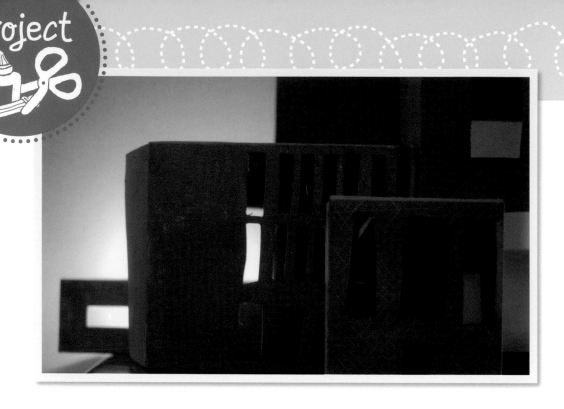

cardboard cityscape

My son's current passion is anything related to architecture; he's been fascinated by structures for the past year or so. And I love repurposing things, especially from the recycle bin. So why not make a wee city or neighborhood out of old cardboard packaging? I also hoped that by adding some after-dark lighting to the cityscape, it may help us chase away those pesky monsters that have been frequenting our home as of late.

materials

* Assorted cardboard packaging boxes
* White acrylic paint
* Paste Paper Mixture (see What Is Paste Paper Mixture? on page 97)
* Cellophane
* Glue dots
* Brads

tools

* Paintbrushes
* Craft utility knife
* Fork
* Scissors
* Battery-operated tea lights

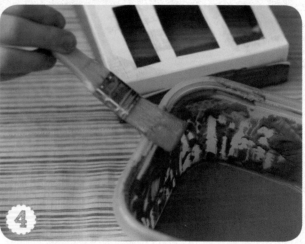

technique

1 Help your child imagine and sketch a city that he or she would like to build. Use that sketch to then gather boxes in varying sizes that suit the sketches. Plan where each box is going, and decide where to put the windows and doors. Include these ideas in your sketch.

2 Apply a coat of white paint to all the boxes and let them dry, at least 30 minutes. While the paint is drying, create the Paste Paper Mixture as described on page 97. Allow it to cool for a couple of hours.

3 On the front of each box, have your child draw the windows and doors based on the sketches. When

the drawing is complete, cut out the holes with a sharp craft knife (this step should be done by a responsible adult). Also cut out an area in the back of each box to give you room to apply the cellophane and insert the tea light later.

4 Paint the back of the boxes with a liberal application of Paste Paper Mixture and let them dry.

what is paste paper mixture?

Paste Paper Mixture is a substance made from flour and water that is applied onto paper to build texture. Once the substance is on the paper, patterns can be made by marking on it and then allowing it to dry. Here's how you make a batch:

* Bring five cups of water to a rolling boil.

* In a separate bowl, whisk together one cup of flour and one cup of water.

* Whisk the flour and water mixture into the boiling water.

* While it is still hot, pour the mixture through a strainer to remove clumps of flour.

* Divide the mixture into smaller containers and mix in acrylic paints into the mixture to add color. Cover the containers and allow the mixture to cool.

5 Paint the fronts of the boxes with Paste Paper Mixture and before the fronts dry, use a fork to create line textures. The thicker you apply the mixture, the more texture you'll get and, subsequently, the longer it will take to dry. The good side of it taking a while to dry is that you can "erase" your mistakes by running the brush over it and starting your texturing over. Allow the paste paper to fully dry.

6 Cut sheets of cellophane to fit the windows and door holes. Adhere them inside the boxes behind the windows and doors with glue dots.

7 Attach the boxes together with brads: Cut slits into the adjoining boxes and then slip each brad through two adjoining boxes. Two brads per side should be enough. Continue attaching boxes with brads until they are all assembled.

8 Add the battery-operated tea lights to the back of your cityscape to cast a warm glow.

merrilee liddiard

www.mermag.blogspot.com

embracing creativity with children

I think some children are definitely born with a talent for creativity, which should be cultivated. However, I believe all children benefit greatly from being exposed to a world of creativity. There is a great deal that can be taught to kids about creativity, but, in the end, they would have to take it from there.

I find that if I'm excited about creating, my kids are too. However, keeping them engaged for the duration of the creative project can be a challenge. I try to make projects simple, no longer than an hour with multiple breaks (and much shorter for the littler ones). Process is of course important, but I also believe that a project with some sort of visual, colorful, wow-factor in the end helps them feel proud of their efforts. This also helps them to be much more willing to embrace creative endeavors the next time around.

There is a great deal that can be taught to kids about creativity, but, in the end, they would have to take it from there.

a childhood filled with inspiration

My sisters and I were rainy day crafters and artists growing up. My mom got all the old *McCalls*, *Butterick*, and *Simplicity* books when the local fabric stores were done with them. We looked forward to days spent indoors cutting out pictures and pasting them to papers, creating wonderful stories and collages. This was officially coined as "cut and paste" time, which I fell in love with. One of my all-time favorite activities was paper dolls. We would spend countless hours drawing and creating characters, their stories, and the clothing that they would wear.

My mother also had mini classes for us in the summer time, which involved cooking and sewing. I can still remember sewing my own drawstring beach/laundry bag in bright yellow with my initials monogrammed on it. I was very proud of it and would tote it around everywhere. My parents also gave us new coloring books and crayons when they went on special date nights each month. It was a time that we all looked forward to with much eagerness. Needless to say, creativity was alive and thriving in my household as a child.

a therapeutic process

I've started to keep a collection of old clothing to be reused as fabric for random craft, sewing, and quilt projects. I love how it not only saves money, but also makes the end product so much more personal. It brings a history to the new work, which gives it depth alongside the fresh energy of the piece.

I also like to hunt for vintage '70s stationery or school paper. You can find some really cool pieces, and I love the different things you can do with them. And of course we've been known to collect one too many toilet paper or paper towel tubes, and cracker and cereal boxes, with the hope of making them into something new and mind-blowing.

With quilting, I enjoy the process, but I get much more out of looking at and enjoying the end product. I like discovering how it wears with time, seeing my little ones all snuggled up in it time and again, and going back over the little stitches and fabric choices. Other projects, particularly ones that involve painting or some sort of artistic expression, are thoroughly enjoyable in the moment. I enjoy looking at them afterward, but it doesn't do the same thing for me as when I'm in the midst of painting.

kitchen crafts

We've found that even simple creative activities in the kitchen make cooking and eating much more fun. Here are some of our favorites:

* **Crackers and cheese.** We are cracker and cheese enthusiasts, and have explored many creative ways of putting these two edible delights together and presenting them.

* **Cookie cutters.** I'm also a big fan of cookie cutters. Anything can be given a fun and creative edge when stamped out in an animal, letter, or creative shape (and they suddenly get much tastier for little mouths, which is a big plus).

* **Inventive sandwiches.** We also like to "sandwich" everything. For example, there is an amazing amount of delectable edibles that can be placed between a pair of graham crackers, such as cream cheese and apples; chocolate frosting and peanut butter; and ice cream, bananas, and chocolate-hazelnut spread.

crafting your own world

Creation is in all of us. Finding our own inspired ways of exploring, expressing, and contributing it is important for our overall mental health and well being. I'm one of those who can't exist if I don't create. It's just a part of me. If I'm feeling blue or stressed, I find that if I just make something, I feel much better. It's like I have this nervous creative energy swirling around inside of me at all times, and I don't feel calm or content until I do something with it.

When I can't sleep at night, I'm often thinking about all of the many creative ideas I have swirling around in my brain, and trying to decide which ones I should pursue. I'm also often wondering how I should prioritize those creative projects with the rest of my life.

I think part of the gift of creativity is meant to uplift and inspire others, so I feel it's extremely important to share the creative gifts we've been given with others. This can be brought about in many different ways, be it on a blog, as a gift to a friend, in your home all around you, or, most importantly, within your family and with your children.

I've lived a more fulfilled life because of my love of art. There is something magical about creating and crafting my own world. Rather than something solely derived by stores and trends, my life becomes an expression of me.

I also enjoy the process of bite-size sewing/craft projects. Picking out the fabric, feeling and hearing the swish of the scissors while cutting the fabric, and stitching away on the sewing machine are really therapeutic and just plain great.

rainy day crafts

I use my childhood favorites to make a rainy day fun, which could include the following:

❋ **Cutting and pasting.** Magazines and glue sticks are just about the simplest and easiest ways to keep my kids entertained in a crafty way. They could "cut and paste" for hours.

❋ **Soda crate of supplies.** I've also recently put together an old wooden soda crate filled with various crafty/creative supplies to get the wheels turning in my little ones' heads. I just place it down in front of them with a stack of paper and they go at it.

❋ **Baking cookies.** Of course, if all else fails, we bake! We love baking together as a family. Cookies are a surefire winner on any day of the week, rain or shine. Who doesn't love a creative endeavor that involves something scrumptious and sweet at the end?

keepsake pillow

My son recently created a drawing that I really loved on a scrap of paper, and I wanted to keep it forever. The paper wasn't in the best condition and it didn't display his wonderful art in a way that I felt it deserved. I also really wanted to display his work in a unique and permanent way. After some thought, I came up with the idea of stitching his artwork onto fabric to create a keepsake pillow.

I also loved the idea that he could help work on this with me, rather than me doing it alone for him. In the end, it really became a wonderful way to boost his self-confidence, as he saw how something special he created was being taken to the next creative level. Upon seeing the finished pillow, I could see his sense of pride in his creation as he hugged the pillow, grinning from ear to ear. It was altogether a wonderful experience for both of us!

materials

* Paper
* Permanent marker
* Disappearing fabric marker
* 2 matching pieces of fabric for the pillow front, cut to 13 x 17 inches (33 x 43.2 cm)
* 1 piece of coordinating fabric for the pillow back, cut to the same size
* White embroidery floss
* Travel pillow form, 12 x 16 inches (30.5 x 40.6 cm)

tools

* Light table
* Embroidery hoop
* Embroidery needle

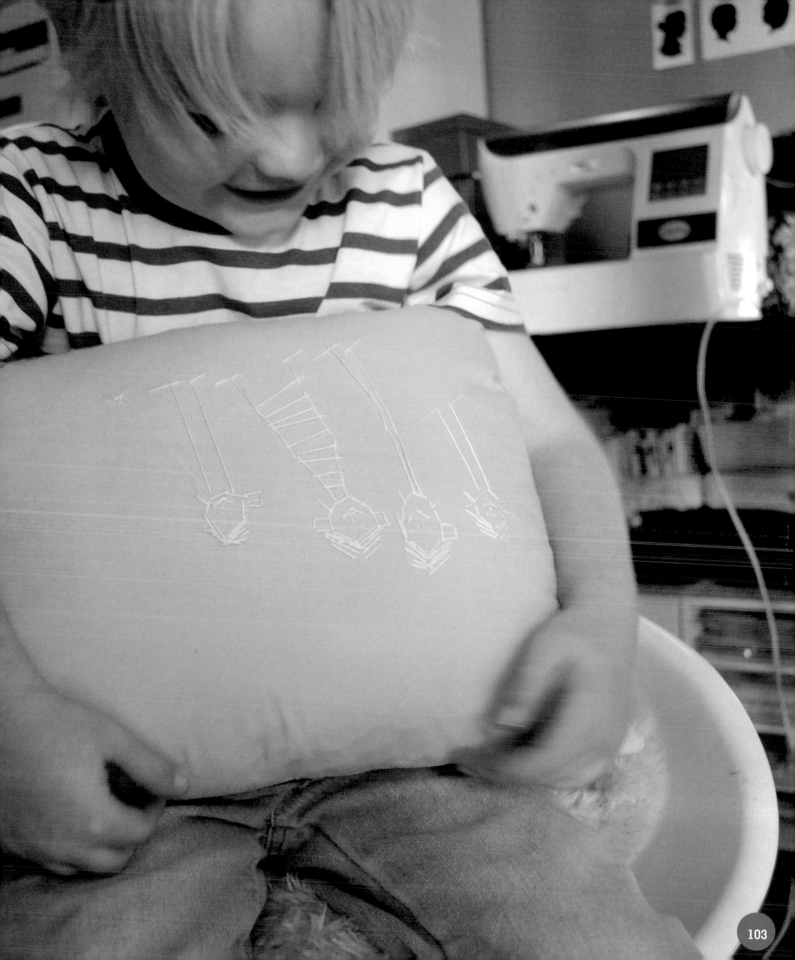

technique

1 Have your children create a drawing of your family using a permanent marker.

2 Next, transfer the artwork onto the fabric using a disappearing fabric marker and a light table. If you do not have a light table, tape the drawing and fabric to a window.

3 Place the fabric with the completed drawing in an embroidery hoop, ready for stitching. Thread a needle with white embroidery floss, tie a knot at the end of the floss, and help your child get started on the first stitch. In the smaller, more detailed parts of the artwork, like the face, you may have to help guide a bit where the needle and floss should go.

It's fun to see your child remember the artwork well enough to have opinions about where the stitches should go.

4 For younger children, teach them a simplified version of the running stitch, where the needle goes up from the backside of the fabric and then back down from the face side of the

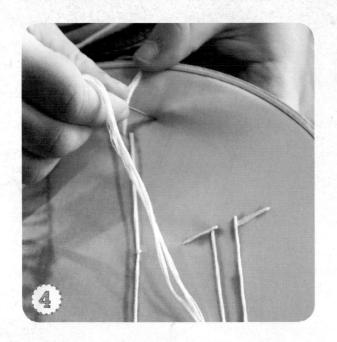

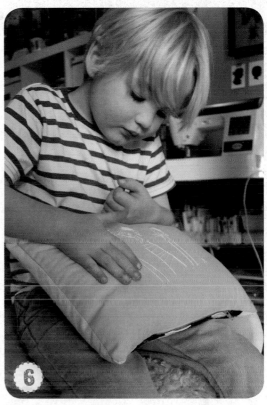

fabric. Even with this simplified up and down running stitch, they will be able to modify their stitches to create tiny eyes and nose and long legs. For older children, gauge their readiness to learn more complex stitches as you introduce them to the back stitch, the French knot, the blanket stitch, and more.

5 When the stitching is complete, remove the hoop. Pin the piece of matching fabric behind the stitched artwork (on the wrong side of the fabric) and baste. This is to prevent snags when pulling the pillow into the case. Dab the fabric with a damp cloth to remove marks from the fabric marker.

6 With right sides facing, pin the stitched pieces to the coordinating fabric. Stitch them together on all sides, leaving a generous opening for inserting the pillow form. Trim the corners and and turn the case right side out. Stuff the pillow form into the case and sew the opening closed. Your child will enjoy watching the artwork come to life!

jhoanna
monte aranez

I encourage my girls to create, to use their hands and make something out of whatever may be on hand at the time, regardless of whatever the end project may be.

time for exploring

Creativity needs to be encouraged and cultivated, just like any other life skill. In order to be creative with your hands, you also need to be able to think creatively; this is an important skill to have in solving daily problems. I encourage my girls to use their hands and make something out of whatever may be on hand at the time, regardless of whatever the end project may be. I ensure that we make time for these kinds of activities—time not just to make, but to experiment, explore, and sometimes just think and talk about ideas. Many of my friends and family members comment on how creative the girls are, but I am certain that if we didn't set aside time for them to be creative, it would not be something they would enjoy and be passionate about.

projects big & small

Just like with my girls, it's important for me to be creating, whether the projects are big or small, and whether I finish them or not. The smallest projects I have worked on are usually something for the home. For example, I make pillowcases for the girls' favorite pillows, which they sleep with at night. These pillows get slept on, stepped on, tossed, thrown, and pulled this way and that, so they wear out. The pillowcases are simple, easy projects, but the girls really appreciate them, especially because they get to choose the fabric.

rainy day crafts

There are periods in Melbourne when it's raining constantly, so it's important for us to know what we can do when it's wet outside. We often refer to our craft cabinet on days like this. The girls know that if there is something they want to make, they can find the materials there. It has all the supplies needed to make beaded jewelry or to paint. There's a special set of fine art crayons and pencils; playdough supplies with associated extras such as shape cutters and pretend kitchen utensils; and stickers, mini pompoms, glitter, glue, sequin shapes, cardboard, and so forth.

The most epic projects I have experienced are, without a doubt, solo exhibitions. Not only do I need to work on the actual toys and dolls and artwork to exhibit, but I have to get the word out and promote, which can be a little stressful, since it's not something that comes naturally to me. For my first solo exhibition in Melbourne, I had about 25 individual pieces. Though there were a few pieces of artwork and photography, the majority were toys and dolls. It was a lot of work, as I was also working full-time at my day job, but it was so rewarding to see them all on display. The feedback and reaction from those who saw it was so wonderful and encouraging.

escaping to my own world

I loved to make things as a child. I remember being five or six and not

having one of those small personal radios that I saw people had on TV. So I got a shoebox, rubber bands, sticky tape, bottle caps, and other odds and ends and made one. It didn't actually play music, but that didn't stop me from pretending that it did.

Growing up, I loved a show called *Play School*. It was on after school and there were a lot of segments on crafting, using typical supplies you could find in your home. I watched this show devotedly and then would go off and make playdough, turn boxes into makeshift dollhouses, and do a ton of paintings and drawings. It was so much fun. This was all on my own, since my mum and dad worked long days, and most days I was home by myself after school for a few hours. My most vivid childhood memories are those that involve making something. It was my way of escaping into my own little world for a while.

plush animal cushion

My girls are very much into cushions and pillows at the moment. Their collection includes licensed products with Disney characters and Dora the Explorer, given to them by family and friends. I thought it would be a great idea for them to have a cushion in the shape of an animal head, since my eldest is starting to show more interest in animals in general.

My eldest is fairly comfortable sewing straight lines on the machine, so when I designed the cushion, I tried to make the lines and shapes as simple as possible so she could help. My youngest helped with sewing on buttons, which is something she had done at her preschool many times. My main contributions were to stitch the two sides of the cushion together and sew the opening closed at the end.

materials

* 1 piece of brown felt, 18 x 8 inches (45.7 x 20.3 cm)

* 1 piece of lavender or pink felt, 18 x 8 inches (45.7 x 20.3 cm)

* Green, white, teal, and orange felt scraps

* 2 buttons for center of eyes

* Fabric spray adhesive

* Polyester fiberfill

tools

* Templates (pages 158–159)

* Scissors

* Pins

* Sewing machine and thread

* Hand-sewing needle

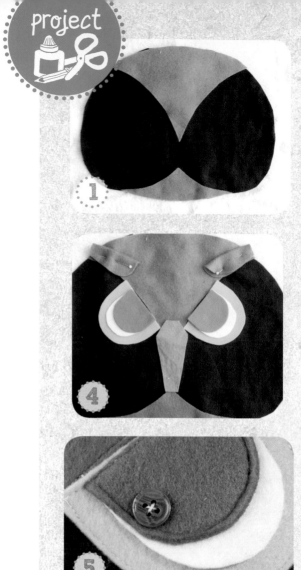

tips & variations

✳ Because the felt can be quite thick, sewing through many layers can be very challenging for a child. Whether this is done by machine or by hand, make sure you are there to help.

✳ Consider adding other embellishments to your cushions, such as ribbons and embroidery.

✳ You could also try lots of other felt color combinations, or even incorporate patches of favorite fabric.

✳ Increase the scale of the pattern to make a larger, more huggable cushion.

technique

1 Cut out each template. All templates come with a ¼-inch (6 mm) seam allowance built in. Pin each template to the correct piece of felt (as labeled on the template) and cut out the pieces, transferring all markings.

2 Check the placement of the upper and lower head pieces on the owl head front, then apply spray adhesive to the back of each piece and press them

in place. Do the same with the beak and eye pieces, stacking the eye pieces one on top of the other.

3 Edgestitch around all the appliquéd pieces to secure them.

4 Fold and pin the bottom of the ears, with the tops of the ears pointing toward the eyes. Baste them in place.

5 To make the owl appear to be looking down, place the buttons in the lower center of each teal eye piece and hand-sew them in place. With right sides facing, pin the front and back head pieces together. Stitch around the outer edge, leaving an opening at the top as marked on the template. Clip and notch the curves, turn the fabric right side out, stuff, and hand-sew the opening closed.

jean
van't hul

www.artfulparent.typepad.com

a rebirth of creativity

I've always been interested in creative pursuits, but I feel like I had a rebirth of creativity when I became a mother. It's as if I birthed more than just a baby; I also birthed a new, more creative me. I started wanting to create for (and later, with) her. I took up sewing again after a decade of not touching a sewing machine. I read books about art and creativity, about adults and children. I started an art group for toddlers when my daughter turned one. My interest in art and creativity, especially children's art and creativity, became an incredibly important part of my life.

Creativity is about originality and imagination, what many of us think of as "outside the box" thinking. It's the ability to transcend the traditional and create meaningful new ideas and things. My efforts as an artful parent will be worth it if my daughters are comfortable with their own creative selves when they grow up. I want them to be at home with the creative process, whether it involves art or music, mathematics or human relations. I want them to own their creativity and apply it to their lives and to also recognize and aid the creative potential of the people and the world around them. I want this for all children, not just my own.

My efforts as an artful parent will be worth it if my daugters are comfortable with their own creative selves when they grow up.

inspiring beyond my family unit

I like to think that I am encouraging others, beyond my immediate family, to be more creative—that I am challenging them to embrace their own originality and resourcefulness and to encourage the same in their children. I'm trying to do this with my children's art groups, my book, my blog, my arts column, and the magazine articles I write. It feels like ripples on a pond. I started out just wanting to try some art with my first child as she became a toddler. But my enthusiasm for children's art and creativity, especially open-ended, process-oriented art, has grown. It's much too big of an idea to keep enclosed in our little family unit.

I love sharing art with small children but what I really, really love is to share the enthusiasm, the inspiration, and the tools with other parents. That way it opens up the creative potential that all families possess. It's the whole idea of "give a man a fish or teach him how to fish." Those parents can keep the love of art and creativity alive in their homes and encourage it in their children regularly, every day. And they can see and experience the joy it brings to their families. I can share art with a child once, or I can share ideas and enthusiasm with the child's parents in the hopes of ensuring an entire childhood (a lifetime, even!) full of art and creativity.

kitchen crafts

As much as I love having an art studio, we really gravitate toward the kitchen and dining room; it's the center of our home. Cooking together is life-affirming, fun, and so appreciated by my older daughter especially.

❋ One of our favorite kitchen crafts is bread dough modeling. We use bread dough to create teddy bear bread, monster bread, bread faces, suns, moons, and flowers. We shape the bread dough as if it were modeling dough, add raisin eyes and decorations as desired, let it rise a bit, brush it with an egg wash, then bake it. It's always a special meal when we eat our own creations. Whether we turn the teddy bear into a sandwich or eat the monster faces with soup, we have as much fun eating them as making them.

❋ We also do most of our color-mixing experiments and make homemade art material in the kitchen. As with cooking, making the paints and other materials is often even more fun than using them. We make watercolors, salt paint, puffy paint, finger paint, play dough, salt dough, and more. Most recipes require simple, inexpensive ingredients that we often already have around the house. Some experiments are more successful than others, but they are all successful in the sense that they are fun and engaging.

engaging children in creativity

Enthusiasm, encouragement, and modeling are essential when teaching creativity to children, but I really think accessible materials are the most important. Children are inspired by what they see and they use what is around them. If markers and paper are left out on the table, visible and available to use, they will get used. If the paints are made available, kids will use them, whether to paint a picture or to add details to their cardboard box fort. If scissors and tape are available for the children's use, they will be used.

Of course, when deciding what to make accessible, you need to keep in mind the ages of your children and what is safe and appropriate. You'll keep the scissors and paints out of reach of your one-year-old, while allowing some well-supervised painting. Really, accessibility

can mean anything from a table dedicated to art, where your art materials can be left out all the time, to a shelf or cupboard where art materials are kept accessible but put away between use. It can be an easel stocked with paints or a bucket of outdoor art materials left on the back porch. Ready access to art materials is the key to engaging children in creative activities.

creative incentive

On a rainy or snowy day, all of us enjoy activities that keep us cozy, safe, and together.

✳ We enjoy baking cookies, muffins, pretzels, popovers, or anything else we might think of. Food warms the body and soul.

✳ We also snuggle up and read more on rainy days.

✳ One favorite craft is to pull out some toothpicks and marshmallows and my five-year-old daughter will build sculptures with them. This will keep her busy for a long time.

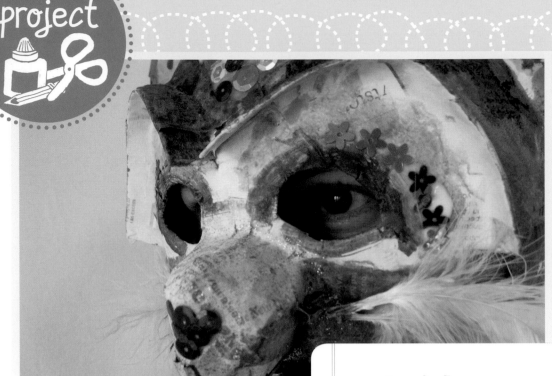

papier-mâché masks

Papier-mâché is a fun, hands-on activity for kids of all ages. We've made everything from bowls and eggs to piñatas and crowns. We did our first project (a large egg) when Maia was two and papier-mâché was as much of a hit with her then as it is now. Dressing up and playing make-believe are daily activities for Maia at the moment, so we've been creating these masks to add to our dress-up collection.

materials

* Newspaper
* Balloons, blown up as large as the child's face, 1 for each mask
* Plastic wrap
* Paper-mâché paste (see the recipe on page 119)
* Cardboard (cereal box, toilet paper rolls, or egg carton)
* Masking tape
* Tempera or acrylic paint
* Mod Podge or acrylic sealer (optional)
* Feathers, yarn, sequins, collage items (optional)
* Glue
* Elastic, long enough to span the back of the head, ¼-inch (6 mm) wide, 1 for each mask

tools

* Two small bowls
* Scissors
* Hole punch
* Paintbrush

1

2

3

4

5

6

technique

1 Cover each bowl with plastic wrap to keep papier-mâché from sticking to the bowls. Blow up the balloon and set it on its side on top of a bowl.

2 Tear the newspaper into strips. Dip a strip of newspaper into the paste, wipe excess off with fingers, and lay the strip on the balloon, smoothing it down.

3 Continue adding more strips with the edges overlapping. Repeat until you have three layers covering half of the balloon. Let this dry completely. This may take a couple of days.

4 Pull the papier-mâché shell off the balloon (or just pop the balloon). Use scissors to trim and even out the edges of the mask.

5 Hold the mask up to the child's face and use a pencil to mark where the eyes are. Use scissors to cut out holes for the eyes, and if desired, for the mouth and nose. Check after cutting to see if the holes are large enough.

6 From cardboard, cut out three-dimensional features such as ears, eyebrows, nose, or a crown. Tape them to the mask as desired.

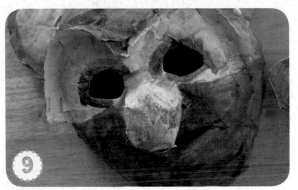

papier-mâché paste recipe

In a medium bowl, whisk together the following ingredients:

✻ 1 cup flour

✻ 2 cups water

✻ 3 tablespoons of salt (to prevent mold if you live in a humid climate)

✻ ½ cup white glue

7 Add another layer or two of papier-mâché strips over the entire mask, especially to the new features, and allow this to dry again.

8 Paint the mask. We use tempera paint, which is more child-friendly and also reveals some of the newspaper beneath (a look that I think adds to the charm of the masks). Use acrylics if you want to conceal the newspaper better.

9 To help protect the mask, you can apply a layer of Mod Podge or acrylic sealer after the paint dries. Let it dry completely overnight.

10 Decorate the mask by gluing on feathers, sequins, yarn, or other collage items.

11 Punch holes at each side of the mask. Tie each end of the elastic to the holes, and try the mask on the child to measure the necessary length.

kristin zecchinelli

www.mainemomma.blogspot.com

when magic happens

I am very fortunate to be able to be a stay-at-home mom at this time in my life. This allows me the opportunity and time to be creative and to stress creativity in my own children's lives. So many children do not have their parents at home to share this with them. Many go to schools where there is little or no funding for art programs. This is truly heartbreaking to me, but of course a reality for so many. Whenever I have a chance to pay it forward, I love to show people how much they can do creatively, using very simple items around their house.

I often wish I had a whole day to spend with a group of kids who do not craft. We would create things from nature, such as paintbrushes made from pine boughs or twigs, nature rubbings with leaves, or drawing tools from rocks. Children can find so much all around, if they are shown where to look. And of course I would bring my camera and allow them to shoot. I find it so fascinating to discover what a child sees through the lens of a camera: what or who they focus on, how they see, what beauty they find.

For my family, I find it essential to create a home environment that encourages individual creativity and play.

becoming their own creative selves

For my family, I find it essential to create a home environment that encourages individual creativity and play. I strongly feel that our home should be very hands-on for our children. They have easy access to art supplies, and free reign as to where they wish to display their art throughout our home. I created a nook with a simple table and chairs where their very own art supplies are stored. Reams of paper, pencils, crayons, child-safe scissors, glue, markers, and tape are all right there for them—all day, every day. It never gets put away. I organize the art supplies from time to time, but it is right in our living room where our family life is centered. They can come and go from this space, knowing that anything they may need to sit and create is right there for them.

It has been interesting to watch my three little ones grow up and become their own creative selves. My eldest daughter, who is soon turning 18, was not as interested in crafting as I had hoped. But then, as she grew, she learned skills that even I don't have. For example, she taught herself to crochet (I have no idea how). Now she is often my teacher, which I find so exciting.

My middle child, my son, was truly born creative. He has been coloring and drawing since he was old enough to grasp a crayon. He now loves all things creative it seems, including painting, drawing, story writing, and working with clay. Art is almost therapeutic to him.

My youngest, my four-year-old girl, is tactile to the max. Everything is done with her hands and in her mouth, so creativity for her has to be tactile. She wants her hands, elbows, hair, or whatever else all right in the thick of it making a beautiful mess. If she has that freedom to make a mess, she loves to create.

a rhythm to our days

Mornings at our house are a time of getting those who are in school off and on to their day. Then as my youngest goes about some playtime, I catch up on my blog and photo work while enjoying my morning cup of coffee. Afternoons are for play and creating up until dinnertime.

Dinnertime is all about the family unit. We eat every dinner together. We cook together. We grocery shop together. I find this to be creative in its own way. For example, my husband likes the process of baking, so he will begin to bake fresh bread and the kids instantly join in the process. It becomes a process we all share in, and we share the fruits of the labor afterward—bonding and creating all at once. I find having a rhythm to our days is essential for us. I find peace in our everyday activities.

tissue paper lanterns

This project came to be by seeing photos of mason jars decorated with lace doilies. I had no doilies around the house, but I did have a stash of fabric scraps and tissue paper. It's a fun project that children of all ages can enjoy.

materials

* White craft glue
* Water
* Tissue paper, two or three colors
* Glass jars of any shape and size
* Tea light or votive candle, one per tissue paper lantern

tools

* Washable bowl
* Paintbrush

1

2

3

technique

1 Prepare the glue mixture by squeezing out a good amount of glue into a bowl (about 3 tablespoons will do to start). Add 1 to 2 tablespoons of water to the glue, and stir. This simply dilutes the glue, making it easy to apply with your paintbrush.

2 Tear the tissue paper into varying sizes, no precision necessary. Just rip away! Have fun making a bit of a mess with your paper pieces, and then set them aside.

3 Choose a jar and apply tissue paper to the outside, piece by piece, by spreading a thin layer of your diluted glue on each piece. The paper will absorb the glue. Hands will be sticky, but it all washes off quickly and easily in the end. Layer as many pieces and

Tips

❋ Make crafts at a washable surface in your home, or even outdoors. The glue will inevitably run a bit, especially if your kids are younger and like to be a bit heavy-handed with painting on the glue.

❋ The tissue paper colors may also run a tiny bit from the drips of glue, but it will easily wash off. There's nothing that warm soapy water won't take care of.

colors as you wish. Each layer adds a new dimension in color. I encourage you to cover all of the glass on the outside of the jar.

4 When you are done applying the papers, set the jar aside to dry fully (approximately 1 to 2 hours).

5 When your lantern is fully dry, trim any excess paper from the rim of the jar. Insert a candle into your jar, and light it. Now the magic happens. The candlelight illuminates the paper you applied, creating a beautiful stained glass effect. Display the lanterns in your home for a beautiful glow.

VARIATION

Instead of tissue paper, you can substitute fabric pieces and apply them the same way to your lantern. The patterns of the fabric will add texture to the filtered light.

ella pedersen

www.littleredcaboose.ca

If I can keep quiet as "Mom" and simply observe and listen, I find myself being the one inspired by my children's raw creativity.

inherently imaginative

As a family, we live most creatively when we schedule less and allow creativity to evolve from those quiet, unplanned times. If I can keep quiet as "Mom" and simply observe and listen, I find myself being the one inspired by my children's raw creativity.

I believe that all children are inherently imaginative and creative forces. As parents and teachers of young children, it's great if we can create a child-friendly space and then step back and allow them to really play there and create. I don't necessarily mean we need to leave the room, but rather work, create, and play alongside without extra chatter and explanation. I know that I step in far more frequently than I know better to, but if I can resist imposing my own

ideas, I find myself being the one inspired in a whole new way. Some children seek and delve into projects more easily, while others require more prompting, but given the opportunity, time, and space, children will imagine and create with gusto.

With little ones, the process of creating is far more essential than any finished product. The art of playing with children is much like an actual child's play. Setting up the show may span the entire morning: setting the stage, finding props and costumes, making a ticket booth, organizing seats, and considering special effects. The actual play might be greatly lacking in content and some days it's more of a rehearsal than an actual show, but there is rarely disappointment.

129

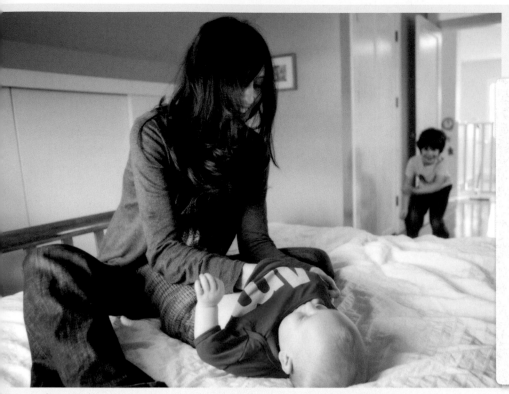

delving & digging for inspiration

As for myself, I do like to have a beautiful finished product, especially if I'm working on a gift for someone. But I also have to love the entire process of creating it, or else there is no point. Puttering about, organizing, and arranging things in my studio is indeed a creative process, if not therapeutic. I am often wishing for more undisturbed daylight hours to spend in the studio pulling fabrics, matching textures and trims, and just playing.

My love of organizing and sifting through things began at a young age. It was fascinating as a child to root through those deep cupboards in the basement rec room, or to climb over stacks of boxes under the stairs into deep, hidden corners where treasures might be found. Often what I found brought forth stories and recollections from my own mama. She grew up on a farm, and when she was not working hard, she had to be creative in her play.

On one of my hunting and gathering expeditions I came across a fascinating quilt top, which my mama and her siblings all hand stitched together; it was made of scrap pieces from the clothing they wore and grew out of. Without a doubt, at that moment I was inspired to begin collecting bits of inspiration, including my own little fabric collection (even though I could not yet sew at the time). When it came to digging, delving, and experimenting, my mama's answer was always, "Yes." I had free run of her sewing room, which was utterly and delightfully cluttered.

happens. "Let's make magic" is code for "Let's turn this upside-down day upside right." Perhaps Mr. Stick needs to go exploring (Mr. Stick is just that: an adopted stick friend who comes exploring with us), or perhaps we should go see if the pond is frozen. I'll say anything to get us outside!

Once we are out there in the fresh air, away from my computer and other distractions, we come together happily. Often I sling my camera alongside my babe so I can photograph our adventures. Other times I take along a knitting bag, just in case the wee one sleeps and the older one is immersed in his own project. Always at some point I take part in the digging or the building and the wondering. Most of the time we end up outside doing much more than we had originally planned to do; maybe we had decided to go out to build a hole, but in the end we've also played tic-tac-toe with sticks and stones, created a shell mosaic, or played pinecone stick ball.

If we have other children in our home for the day, baking bread is a hands-on, sensory rich experience that we love to do. Though it keeps us inside, never have I heard a child refuse the opportunity to bake bread. As soon as we start baking, the home becomes instantly cozy with the oven warming. I sprinkle snowflakes of flour in front of each child where they may "draw" while waiting to receive their ball of dough. We sing as small rounds are passed to each child. "Do you know the baker man?" They may feel the warmth, the weight, and the texture of the dough as they knead and shape it. We like to shape the dough rather than use cookie cutters.

go bag

* Other than a container of snacks, a full water bottle, and diapers, I like to head out with the mantra that less is best. The adventure is the entertainment, especially out of doors.

* If we go to the ocean, we may take a shovel or two, but we often use seashells for scoops too.

* We occasionally bring along a basket to collect small treasures.

* We often carry a tote with a notebook and colored pencils with which to write and make mazes and puzzles.

These days, as I'm puttering around and organizing, many of my favorite projects are ones created specifically for my boys. Much of what I'm creating in my studio is also a reflection of the seasons and our celebrations. Whether from a pattern or my own experiment, I get excited about these little surprise projects, as I anticipate my little ones' delight upon their discovery of a needle-felted witch for our autumn nature table, various advent gifts from the "elves," or felted Easter eggs to hide and seek.

creating rich experiences

Some days are particularly challenging, when everyone's moods, including my own, are sensitive or irritable. This often has a snowball effect on whatever it is that we are trying to accomplish. If I catch the cue early enough and muster up the oomph to get us all outside and onto a trail or to the ocean, then magic

felt flower bowl

This is a fun project using a wet felted technique. Depending on the age and ability of the child you are creating with, you may each make your own bowl, or you may want to work on one at a time together.

materials

* Wool roving, at least two complementary colors
* Round or egg-shaped solid form
* Rubber band
* Fabric marker

tools

* Water station—a space with hot water and liquid soap
* Felting board (or a sushi mat or bubble wrap)
* Sharp craft knife
* Scissors

beki lambert

www.artsycraftybabe.typepad.com

Failure isn't always a bad thing. Even if a project doesn't work out, I'm still learning along the way.

an artsy-crafty babe

There has never been a time when creativity wasn't a part of my life; it's just always been there. I watched my mom and maw-maw make clothes for me and crochet afghans, I listened to my dad's excellent stories and made-up songs on the guitar, and I learned that my paw-paw could build just about anything. Once I started school, I was fascinated by all the colorful school supplies: crayons, markers, wooden beads, colorful laces, and clay provided me with limitless opportunities for creative play. I anxiously awaited each issue of *Highlights* magazine, so I could make the crafts in the "Things to Make" section. Even as a little kid, I was truly an artsy-crafty babe.

joyful anticipation

Before blogging, my projects would come in phases. It wasn't until I started blogging that I started creating on a regular basis, and now those phases overlap each other to the point that I'm always working on something. I've finally accepted that this is how my brain works. When I'm faced with a situation, usually the first thing I think of is, "How can I make XYZ?"

It is during the planning and making of a project that I feel that rush of adrenaline and joyful anticipation. I love to look back and see how something I'm working on has evolved. I'll often start a project, tweak a thing or two, then move onto something else, but the influence of that last project is still there. I see this most in my appliqué work, which I love.

Failure isn't always a bad thing. Even if a project doesn't work out, I'm still learning along the way. Having spent most of my life in fear of failure, I now realize how much this has held me back. I don't want my kids to make that same mistake.

connecting creatively

Everyone is born creative to some degree, but I believe our environment plays a role in bringing that out. Looking at my own kids, they each have different creative interests. I think it is my role as a parent to experiment with them to find out what suits them best.

One thing we love to do together is paint. It is such a freeing activity because there is no wrong or right way to do it. We mainly use watercolors, for easy clean-up. Periodically, I'll buy inexpensive canvases at the art store for us to make paintings to add to our collection. Our hall bathroom, with its long expanse of wall, has turned into a family art gallery with all our canvas paintings.

When we sit and paint as a family, we inevitably talk and laugh along the way. I love that creative projects allow us to have this time together. Family, the relationships with people in your life, and the experiences you have with them are what matter most. It's not about the stuff you have or the house you live in; it's all about the connections.

kitchen crafts

* I've always let my children participate in the fun things, like decorating cookies and such, but it hasn't been until recently that we've ventured beyond that. Now that my oldest daughter is responsible enough to take charge, I've been letting her make easy meals for the family.

* In the past, I must admit having the kids "helping" in the kitchen was a bit stressful for me. Now, with Lily taking the reigns (under my watchful eye), I'm able to let go of that control a bit. It is still very much a group effort, as the younger ones are much more observant of their older sister in the kitchen than they are of me.

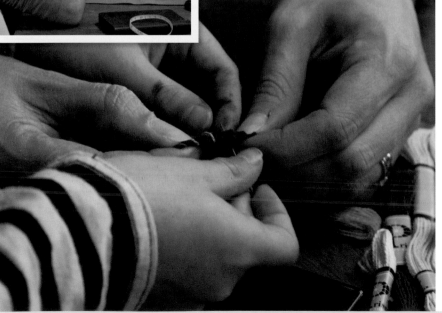

personal electronics pouch

One Christmas, all three of my children received some form of personal game electronics. I thought it would be a good idea for them to make something personalized to hold these new toys. This is an easy project that doesn't have a lot of steps. I did the measuring, cutting, and sewing on of the buttons, but they did the rest. I was very impressed at their hand-sewing skills, especially my six-year-old son. My four-year-old daughter was also very into the sewing aspect of the project. Having the punched holes for them to follow made a big difference.

You could make this pouch for just about anything. After completing our project, my oldest daughter wanted to make another, so she made a small coin pouch. She already has plans to make one for her friend.

materials

* Felt sheets large enough to wrap around your personal electronics, and extras for creating embellishments

* Embroidery floss

* 1 button, any size

tools

* Tape measure

* Scissors and/or pinking shears

* Embroidery needle, or large yarn needle for younger children

* Hole punch (for younger children)

* Glue

* Markers

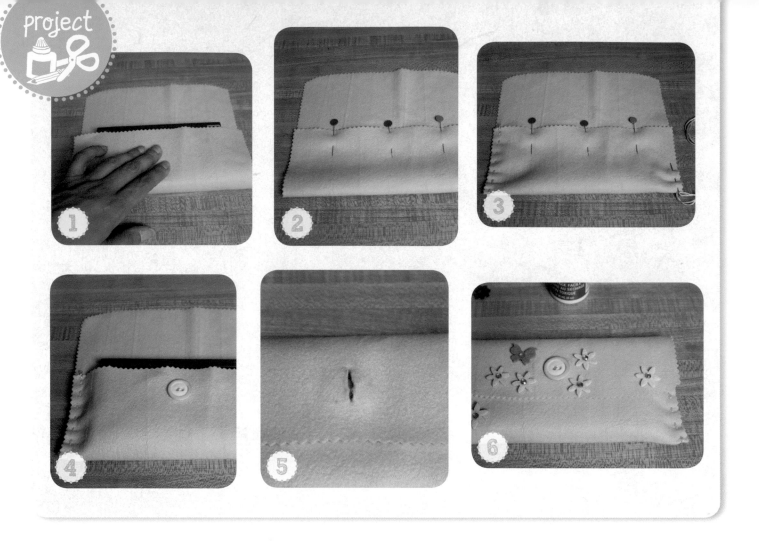

technique

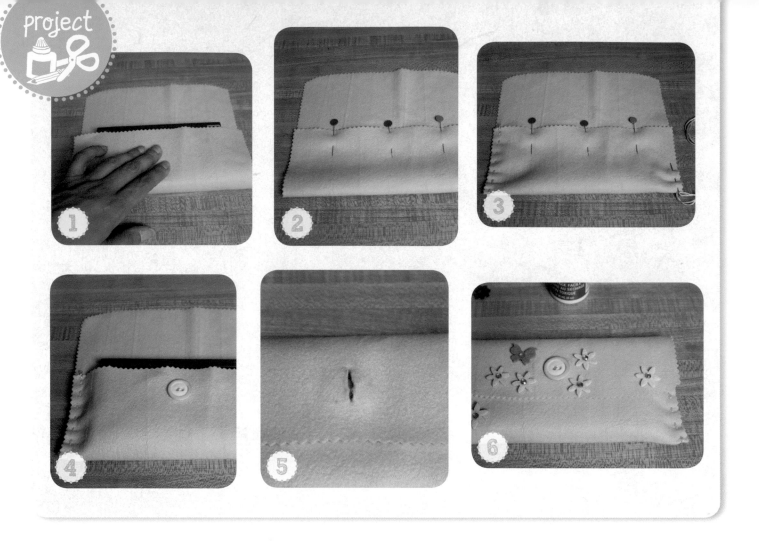

1 To figure out the size of the pouch:
- For the width, measure horizontally around your electronic item: start the measuring tape at one side, then wrap across the top and around the back, returning to where you started. Divide that number in half, then add 1½ inches (3.8 cm) to the number.
- Measure vertically by starting at the top edge and wrapping down the bottom, around the back, back to the top, and down the middle front (to allow for a flap).

- Using these two measurements, cut a piece of felt with regular scissors or with a pair of pinking shears for a decorative edge.

2 Wrap the felt around the electronic item so one edge of the felt is near the top. Remove the personal electronic game and pin the felt to keep the bottom fold of the pouch in place.

3 Starting at the bottom fold, hand sew along the side of the pouch up to the opening using an embroidery needle and floss. When you reach the top front edge, tie off the floss. Repeat on the other side.

4 Sew a large button at the center of the open edge of the pouch.

5 Fold the top of the pouch over to mark the placement of the button, then cut a vertical slit the same size as the button.

6 Now comes the fun part: the decorating! Personalize your pouch by attaching bits of felt with glue, sewing on more buttons, and/or drawing on the felt with markers.

tips

❋ For a younger child, you can punch holes along the side of the pouch using a hole punch. The child can then use a blunt yarn needle to thread embroidery floss through the holes.

❋ Skip the craft felt. It is worth it to splurge on wool or wool-blend felt. We have also used eco-friendly bamboo felt, which was very nice.

jenny doh

www.crescendoh.com

weathering the storms with art

There is not a person in the world who is immune from the dark clouds of life. Accidents, illness, and disappointments happen to all of us. When those clouds get dark, you have to find a way to weather them. What I know for sure is that creative work is the most powerful way for me to weather the storm clouds.

I certainly lived through the storm clouds when I was a young mother, desperate at times to find balance and retain my own voice. It's lonely as heck at 2:00 a.m., when you are nursing, your body is sagging, it's dark, and no one is there to say you're doing a fantastic job. It's when you can knit something cool, quilt something beautiful, grow a tomato, or do anything creative that the sun starts shining through those clouds to remind you that everything is going to be okay.

I hope I've imparted to my kids the significance of creative work in their lives, especially during those hard times. I think it all starts by modeling good behavior. I know I can't get my kids to appreciate handmade crafts unless I model for them the process of making things by hand. Same goes for reading, eating right, and exercising. Parents lead the way through their behaviors, both for young children, who will literally mimic and copy, and for older teens, who will be inspired to follow suit, even if they might be too cool to admit it.

letting kids be who they are

Neither my husband nor I can throw or catch a ball. We are not athletes. Growing up, I was definitely considered more of a nerd, as I stayed home to bake cookies rather than go out and party, or play the cello rather than volleyball. My husband was the same way. Two nerds happily married to each other. Not surprisingly, we created two children who, like us, can't throw or catch. My son, Andrew, was a toddler when we tried to have him do the whole Little League thing. We just thought that in this sports-oriented culture, we ought to have him fit the mold. And boy oh boy, was he unhappy; every time we had to go to a game or practice, it was like he was having to put on an ill-fitting uniform as he obediently marched out into the field, dreading any association with a ball that might come his way.

One day it dawned on me that there is no law that says he has to be in little league. So what if all the other boys were in it? Andrew has never been interested in sports. He is happy as a clam when he has paper, glue, clay, and paints in front of him. My daughter, Monica, is similar in that she has never been interested in sports. She's more of a creative writer and budding actress. The biggest lesson

It's when you can knit something cool, quilt something beautiful, grow a tomato, or do anything creative that the sun starts shining through those clouds to remind you that everything is going to be okay.

technique

1 Sand the wooden beads with sandpaper and wipe them clean.

2 With a foam brush, apply a layer of Mod Podge onto a paper scrap that is large enough to entirely cover one bead.

3 Place the bead onto the paper and wrap the paper around it. Add more Mod Podge if needed. There will be many wrinkles and folds that get created,

which adds character to the beads. Set aside the beads for approximately one hour to dry.

4 Feel through the paper for the bead holes, and poke the wire into one end of the bead and out the other.

5 Use round-nosed pliers to create a loop at the top and bottom of the bead to secure it. Feel free to make loops as large or small as you like.

6 Fold a piece of scrap paper and cut it into the shape of a leaf. Adhere the leaf onto the wire with Mod Podge.

7 Optionally, attach small beads and pearls at the top and bottom loops with fine-gauge craft wire.

8 Once you have completed a bouquet, tie them with a ribbon or place them into a small jar.

rachel faucett

www.handmadecharlotte.com

creating an everyday event

As a child, I never stopped doodling. I don't think of art as something that you pull out on rainy days. Creating is an everyday event. It is always on my mind and never goes away. Inspiration comes from everywhere; I know we've all heard that a million times before, but it is so true. The color of a street sign, the shape of a tree—I get ideas from everything and everywhere.

My mother is an idea factory. My earliest creative memories are with my mom. Not only is she an amazing knitter, but she would also make gigantic candles, plaster sculptures, tie-dye projects, and anything else she could get her hands on. I owe every creative thought I've ever had to my incredible mother.

Creating is an everyday event. It is always on my mind and never goes away.

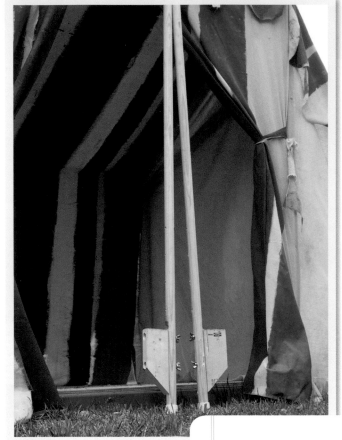

DIY stilts

Stilts hold wonder for a small child; they often lead to make-believe stories and fun playtime. To more easily walk on the stilts, step onto the stilts while backed up against a wall or have someone hold the stilts for you. Like anything, learning how to walk on stilts takes lots of practice. But once you get the hang of it, it's so much fun that you won't want to stop.

* Keep stilt play safe by walking on grass or another soft surface until you get the hang of things!

materials

* Lumber:

   • one 2 x 4, 15½ inches (39.4 cm) long

   • 2 poles, each 1½ inches (3.8 cm) in diameter and 96 inches (243.8 cm) long

* 4 carriage bolts, ⅜ x 4 inches (.95 x 10.2 cm)

* 4 ID flat washers, ⅜ inch (.95 cm)

* 4 wing nuts, ⅜ inch (.95 cm)

* 2 rubber leg tips, 1½ inches (3.8 cm) in diameter

tools

* Saw

* Drill

* Wing bit: ¾ inch (1.9 cm)

* Drill bit: ⅜ inch (.95 cm)

technique

PART 1: THE FOOTHOLDS

1 Cut the 2 x 4 in half at a 45-degree angle, creating two trapezoids. The parallel sides of each should be 6 inches (15.3 cm) and 9½ inches (24.2 cm). These two pieces will form the footholds.

2 On the shorter side of the footholds, bore two holes 1½ inches (3.8 cm) deep with a ¾-inch (1.9 cm) wing bit. Space the holes 4 inches (10.2 cm) apart, center to center.

3 With a ⅜-inch (.95 cm) drill bit, finish drilling the holes all of the way through. This will complete the footholds.

PART 2: THE POLES

1 Drill eight ⅜-inch (.95 cm) holes in both of the 96-inch-long (243.8 cm) pieces of lumber. Start 6 inches (15.2 cm) from the bottom and drill a hole every 4 inches (10.2 cm), until you are 34 inches (86.4 cm) from the bottom.

2 To attach the footholds, insert the carriage bolts through the cut 2 x 4 and the pole, followed by the washers and wing nuts on the other side of the pole. It's best to start out at the lowest height.

3 To prevent the bottom of the poles from splintering, you can attach a 1½-inch rubber leg tip to the end of each pole. These are commonly available to keep the feet of furniture from scratching the floor.

Mother's love is peace.
It need not be acquired,
it need not be deserved.

—Erich Fromm

photo credits

Kathrin Achenbach: 16–20

Arnold Aranez: 106–110

Jackie Boucher: 5

Allyson Brewer: 136–131

Chris Brice: 82–89

Thea Coughlin: 60–64, 66

Jenny Doh: 14–15, 22, 38, 65, 146

Maya Donenfeld: 16–20

Pam Garrison: 32–39

Abby Glassenberg: 46–49

Ali Edwards: 24–31

Chris Edwards: 24–31

Jonathan Faucett: 148–156

Todd Fong: 74–78

Lenka Hattaway Photography: 4, 5, 112–115

Jennifer Haugh: 68–73

Cindy Hopper: 68–73

Amger Johanson: 68–73

Adrian Mandy: 5, 90–97

Robert Moncrief: 2, 98–105

Jessica Okui: 80–81

Ella Pedersen: 5, 128–135, 156

Leanne Pedersen: 5, 128–135, 156

Rachel Penman Photography: 1, 52–59

Kiley Redhead: 5, 90–97

Cynthia Shaffer: 2, 21–23, 43, 45, 50–51, 79, 111, 142–147

Amanda Blake Soule: 8–15

Steve Soule: 8–15

Nicole Spring: 41–42, 44

Kevin Spring: 40

Jean Van't Hul: 4, 5, 112, 116–119

Kristin Zecchinelli: 6, 120, 122–127

Taylor Zecchinelli: 121

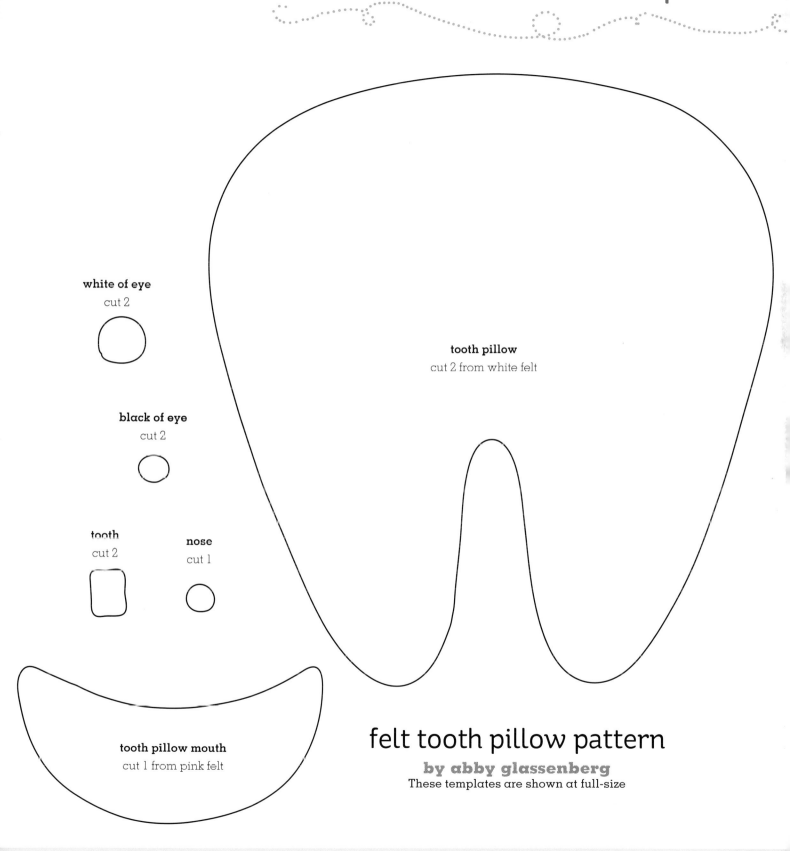

white of eye
cut 2

black of eye
cut 2

tooth
cut 2

nose
cut 1

tooth pillow
cut 2 from white felt

tooth pillow mouth
cut 1 from pink felt

felt tooth pillow pattern
by abby glassenberg
These templates are shown at full-size

templates

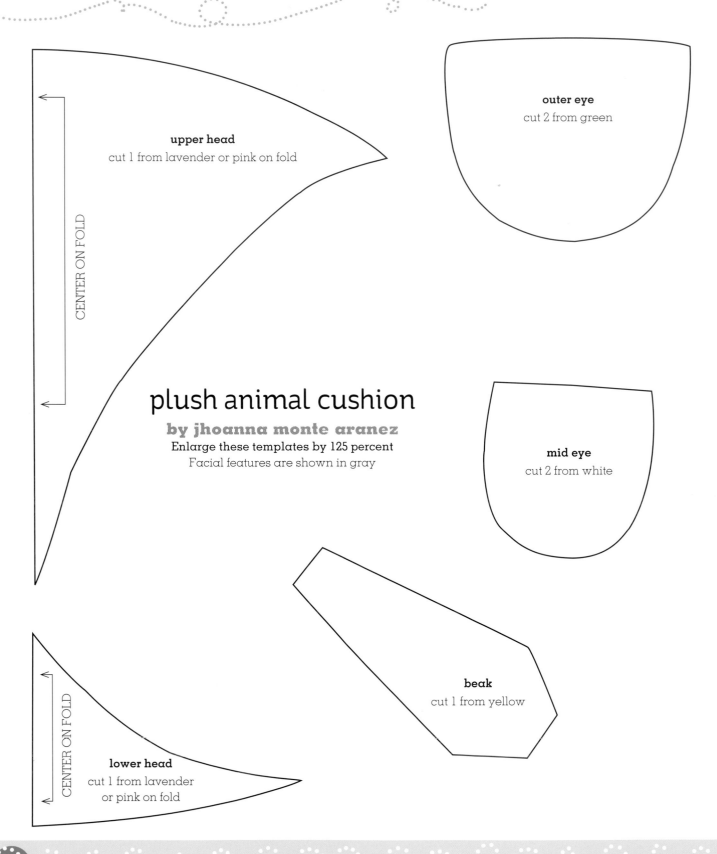

outer eye
cut 2 from green

upper head
cut 1 from lavender or pink on fold

CENTER ON FOLD

plush animal cushion
by jhoanna monte aranez
Enlarge these templates by 125 percent
Facial features are shown in gray

mid eye
cut 2 from white

beak
cut 1 from yellow

CENTER ON FOLD

lower head
cut 1 from lavender
or pink on fold